# *INSIDE COLLEGE*
## New Freedom, New Responsibility

### HENRY C. MOSES

College Entrance Examination Board
New York

*For Mary Sarah Holland,
who is in a class by herself
and*

*In memory of my mother,
who was eager for me to get to college*

In all of its book publishing activities the College Board endeavors to present the works of authors who are well qualified to write with authority on the subject at hand and to present accurate and timely information. However, the opinions, interpretations, and conclusions of the authors are their own and do not necessarily represent those of the College Board; nothing contained herein should be assumed to represent an official position of the College Board or any of its members

Copies of this book are available from your local bookseller or may be ordered from College Board Publications, Box 886, New York, New York 10101. The price is $10.95 plus $2.95 for handling.

Editorial inquiries concerning this book should be directed to Editorial Office, The College Board, 45 Columbus Avenue, New York, New York 10023-6992.

Copyright © by Henry C. Moses. All rights reserved.

Library of Congress Catalog Number: 90-080610

ISBN: 0-87447-383-7

Printed in the United States of America

# Contents

Anticipating................................................... 1
1 Leaving Home, with Baggage ....................... 9
2 Feeling Like a Small Fish in a Big Pond ........ 25
3 Dormitory Living......................................... 35
4 Living with the Rules................................... 47
5 Reading the Course Catalog and Syllabus ..... 63
6 Taking Courses ........................................... 77
7 Looking Into a College Course..................... 89
8 Finding Advice and Counsel.......................101
9 Regarding the Faculty ...............................117
10 Choosing a Major .....................................133
11 Making Extracurricular Commitments ........149
12 Keeping Your Mind Open..........................169
13 Becoming Entangled..................................185
14 Threading the Administrative Maze............199
15 Shaping Your Own Education....................215
Index .......................................................231

# Acknowledgments

page 1, Ralph Waldo Emerson. "Experience," in *Selections from Ralph Waldo Emerson.* Boston: Houghton Mifflin, 1957, p. 261; "Love's Recovery," by Emily Saliers, © 1989, Virgin Songs, Inc./Goodhap Music. All rights reserved. Used by permission; E. B. White. *Charlotte's Web.* New York: Harper, 1952, p. 184.

Chapter 1, *The Education of Henry Adams.* New York: Random House, 1931; Judy Garland as Dorothy in *The Wizard of Oz.* Metro-Goldwin-Mayer, 1939.

Chapter 2, Henry David Thoreau. *Walden.* New York: W. W. Norton, 1966.

Chapter 3, Mark Twain. *The Adventures of Huckleberry Finn.* New York: W. W. Norton, 1962, p. 95; lyrics from "You're Kind," by Paul Simon. © 1975 by Paul Simon; From The Poetry of Robert Frost edited by Edward Connery Lathem. Copyright 1916, 1930, 1939, © 1969 by Holt, Rinehart and Winston. Copyright 1944 by Robert Frost. Copyright © 1967 by Lesley Frost Ballantine. Reprinted by permission of Henry Holt and Co., Inc.

Chapter 4, Lewis Carroll. *Through the Looking Glass.* In, *The Complete Works of Lewis Carroll.* New York: Random House, 1936, pp. 250–51.

Chapter 5, Stanley Cavell. *The Claim of Reason.* New York: Oxford University Press, 1979, p. 120; Emily Dickinson. *Final Harvest.* Boston: Little, Brown and Company, 1961, p. 267.

Chapter 6, "The Divinity School Address." In *Selections from Ralph Waldo Emerson.* Boston: Houghton Mifflin, 1957, p. 104.

Chapter 7, John Keats. "Ode to a Grecian Urn."

Chapter 9, Geoffrey Wolff. *The Duke of Deception.* New York: Berkley, 1980, p. 32; William Butler Yeats. "Among School Children."

Chapter 10, From The Poetry of Robert Frost edited by Edward Connery Lathem. Copyright 1916, 1930, 1939, © 1969 by Holt, Rinehart and Winston. Copyright 1944 by Robert Frost. Copyright © by Lesley Frost Ballantine. Reprinted by permission of Henry Holt and Company, Inc.

Chapter 11, Wallace Stevens, "The Idea of Order at Key West"; Bernard De Koven. *The Well-Played Game.* New York: Anchor/Doubleday, 1978, p. 115; "Tradition and the Individual Talent." In *Selected Essays of T. S. Elliot.* New York: Harcourt, Brace & World, 1964, p. 4.

Chapter 12, Ludwig Wittgenstein. *Philosophical Investigations.* Oxford: Basil Blackwell, 1968, p. 178; Henry David Thoreau. *A Week on the Concord and Merrimack Rivers.* New York: Signet/NAL, 1961, p. 236.

Chapter 14, T. S. Elliot, "Coriolan."

Chapter 15, J. R. R. Tolkein. *The Hobbit.* New York: Houghton Mifflin, 1966, p. 215; Charles Fried. *Right and Wrong.* Cambridge, MA: Harvard University Press, 1978, p. 150; Herman Melville. *Moby Dick or the White Whale.* Cambridge, MA.: Houghton Mifflin, 1956.

*To finish this moment, to find
the journey's end in every step
of the road, to live the greatest
number of good hours, is wisdom.*
                              (Emerson)

*There I am in younger days, star-gazing,
Painting picture-perfect ways of how my
life and love would be
Not counting this unmarked paths of mis-
direction
My compass, faith in love's perfection
I missed ten million miles of road I should
have seen.*
                        (The Indigo Girls)

*She was in a class by herself. It is not often that
someone comes along who is both a true friend
and a good writer. Charlotte was both.*
                              (E. B. White)

# *Anticipating*

This book is intended to inspire both daydreaming and careful thinking about college. It won't tell you how to get into the college of your choice, but it may help you choose more wisely. It won't tell you how to get through an interview satisfactorily either, or how to compose your essays or complete your applications, but read it as you think about doing those things. The book is meant to help you imagine what college is going to be like, as you prepare to leave home and high school, and will allow you to gauge what you already know about college and anticipate some of the challenges you may face.

Just now you may be asking yourself: Will I be able to leave home? Will I be able to make friends? Will I be good enough at anything? What will I major in? Questions like these, extremely important and often on your mind, demand one-word answers. They don't afford you much leeway and may keep you from using your imagination. A book like this one is called for because, though many young people coming to college have asked themselves these hard-line questions, they haven't asked themselves other, more leisurely questions about what lies ahead. Some students do mull over questions that are more open-ended, and their transition from high school seems easier as a result; other students, though, can use some help imagining what college will be like. This book tells stories that ask thought-provoking questions, both directly and indirectly, about what you might look forward to. You don't need to answer any of these questions right away, of course, but just asking them may let you look ahead to some specific situations you wouldn't have thought about otherwise.

## **LET'S THINK ABOUT IT: SOME QUESTIONS**

Before getting to the stories, try out some of the questions that follow. They are not a program for "knowing yourself," just background for decisions you'll eventually have to make.

- What do you like to think or learn about that might become the central interest of your college work: abstract ideas, real

people and real social problems, the remote past, the next hundred years, foreign cultures, scientific or geographical discoveries? (Notice that this is not a question about what you might major in.)
- How would you rate your own skill at reading and writing? How comfortable are you with numbers? Down deep, are you a word person or a number person, or both? How accurately do your grades and scores represent your interests? Have your teachers been astute in their evaluations of you? Do you evaluate yourself differently?
- How do you learn best? Do you try to figure out what a teacher wants and produce it? Do you like details or the "big picture"? Would you rather work on a single, isolated problem or try to see patterns and relationships among problems? What are your intellectual weaknesses? What are your strengths? Are you interested in what you read and write? Do you believe in your own ideas? How clear and fair are your arguments in essays or discussions? Do you know how to give credit to others for their ideas? Can you keep the ideas of others from dominating your own thinking and writing?
- How observant are you likely to be of your college, your teachers, your fellow students, and yourself? Will you be curious about how things work and who does what? How considerate and caring are you, usually? How about when the pressure is on? Can you stay open to others even if they are different from you? Will you give something of yourself to other people in college? Will you be able to find a balance between giving and taking, competing and cooperating? What if college doesn't live up to your expectations? Will you be able to examine your expectations from time to time?
- What sort of leader are you? How good a follower are you? If you don't think of yourself in these terms, how do you characterize the way you relate to others in a group?
- What do you want life in college to feel like? What will make you happy? What will make you unhappy?
- How do you anticipate managing your life in college and taking responsibility for what happens? What do you want the quality of your life there to be?

These questions reach in many directions. They are about ideas and thinking, tolerance and responsibility, institutional and personal politics, and feelings. As I think about the questions, I realize how interested I have become in the ways students express their purposes. But I have also learned that it is possible to press questions of purpose too hard. Not long ago, I was adviser to a freshman who in February brought her spring course program to me showing four courses in sociology. Since we had talked all fall about how important it was to explore wide and deep, especially in the first year, I asked her why she had listed the courses she had. Her answers didn't seem to satisfy even her, so I finally asked point-blank what she wanted from college. She burst into tears.

Might this conversation have gone better if she had asked herself the questions? Perhaps. Will this book prevent tears? Tears will be shed no matter what is in books, but you can hope that there will be words and pictures here to help you understand where the tears come from.

You will experience a degree of freedom in college that will sometimes exhilarate you and may sometimes surprise you with its weightiness. Freedom will be the most powerful force in the transition from high school to college, and you will learn something about responsibility in the face of it. In this connection, there are two challenges that are particularly worth thinking about. How you meet them will affect how you live in college. The first challenge is to stay open to the varied, sometimes even disturbing, points of view of others without letting up on your efforts to find and clarify your own point of view. The second is to be prepared at every turn to take specific responsibility for your decisions and actions. You probably already have a framework or tradition within which to think about all of this, but you may not have thought about college in this way.

## Discovering Yourself

There will be times when you have to think about the nature and purposes of your education. You may come to understand that one of the reasons for pursuing a college education is to become a larger person—broader, deeper, and stronger in mind and spirit. By learning what the great thinkers and their critics have said over the centuries, you will begin the process of identifying what you cherish and where you stand, and ultimately know yourself better. Then, when you take a position on an issue, as members of college communities are often asked to do, you will be able to say why you have chosen that view. You will argue more forcefully and be understood more clearly by others. If you come to see your education this way, the subject you major in will seem much less important than whether you continue to learn to look at things in a carefully reasoned way, exercising good judgment and respecting others. If you learn to do all of this well, you will be all the more prepared to go on to more adult roles.

On virtually a daily basis, you will be challenged to be responsible and fair-minded by quite ordinary college situations. For example, since ideas are the stuff of college reading and writing, honesty about the sources of ideas is required. This is not a mechanical question of footnotes and bibliographies; unless teachers can trust that the work they get from you belongs to you, their evaluations of your work are meaningless.

Giving instructors work that is your own so they can evaluate it accurately is obviously important in college, but, more generally, being clear about what belongs to you and what belongs to others will also be a concern. College may be the first time you have had to share space, furnishings, belongings, and schedules with people outside your family. You won't be able to make the same assumptions about privacy and ownership you could at home. Your roommates may not value the same things you do, so you will sometimes have to negotiate with them. This is not always easy. You will have to speak up and try to be friendly yet firm. You may have to give up some things in order to achieve more important goals.

## . . . And Others

It's also likely that the people in your college will be from different ethnic groups and races, and economic backgrounds, and will hold different political views. The challenge here will be whether you can accept people on their own terms, even though their backgrounds and attitudes are different from yours, and avoid forcing your terms on them.

You can also expect academic and ethical concerns to become intertwined: You will find that certain questions of community keep coming up—about academic honesty and social conduct; differences in race, ethnicity, class, gender, and sexual orientation; and the quality of relationships. The intellectual tone of your college will begin to sound hollow unless people respect one another and themselves; keeping the intellectual tone rich will be important to your own growth.

With some thought and planning, you can shape your college education and experience. Remember, though, that all the lists, descriptions, explorations, claims, arguments, prescriptions, predictions, revelations, opinions, and sermons in this book come from a vantage point that is probably different from your own. To measure the differences in perspective you'll have to know some things. The author is middle-aged, white, male, Calvinist Protestant, the product of a large Eastern public high school and an all-male Ivy League college. He graduated from college early in the sixties (the fifties hadn't really ended yet). He has been a college English teacher and dean for more than 20 years, working in turn at a land-grant university, a university in the South, a small Ivy League university, an even smaller formerly Roman Catholic women's college, and a large urban university. Two of his children have left for college in the past several years. Perhaps surprisingly, truths for them have been truths for him.

The years since the early sixties encompass revolutionary changes in certain aspects of college life. Prior to 1970, there seemed to be more agreement among students about the value and purpose of college. Now people come from such diverse directions and traditions and have such different goals that we cannot take consensus for granted. College life at its best has always been intense, critical, and argumentative because of differences among students, but now students educate one another in ways unheard of before 1970.

So don't assume that this book can describe exactly how things will be for you as you approach college. And although what you will read here is based on careful assumptions and generalizations, you should feel free to challenge them. As you read about this college-going adventure, be curious and imaginative. Other people have gone through experiences similar to those you will go through in the next couple of years. In many ways, you are not alone. Let your family read this book with you and find ways of talking together about the prospect of college. So much of what lies immediately ahead will involve and affect your family that it's good to begin talking about it early.

## ABOUT THIS BOOK

A word or two about the shape of the chapters that follow. Each chapter title names a task or challenge. About the epigraphs, feel free to scratch your head or smile (or both). They suggest ways of approaching the topics of the chapters. From time to time in the body of a chapter, a student will be quoted. When this happens you will be reading an excerpt from a letter a student has sent to me looking back over his or her first year in college. Knowing the way people who are actually in college feel about the topics in this book will be valuable for you, the reader.

I owe thanks to each of the students whose letters I use in this way, to the other students who have taught me, and to my college-bound children, Jim, Bruce, and Paige. Thanks as well to the colleagues and friends who have helped me think and write: Doug Stone, Bob Mortimer, Mindy Davis, Georgene Herschbach, Richard Marius, Loring Conant, John DuVivier, Mark Van Baalen, Mack Davis, Liz Keeney, Will Marquess, Adriana Salerno, Deb Hughes Hallett, Bob Woollacott, Ron Calabrese, Chris Cozzens, Carolyn Trager, Larry and Kim Buell, Howard Stone, and (especially) Karen Heath and Aaron Lemonick.

*Any other education would have required serious effort, but no one took Harvard College seriously. All went there because their friends went there, and the College was their ideal of social self-respect.*
(Henry Adams)

*Toto, I have a feeling we're not in Kansas any more.*
(Dorothy)

# 1
# *Leaving Home, with Baggage*

The college journey can be high adventure—a new experience, full to bursting with meaning for your future. You may already realize that there is no well-defined beginning of the journey (on a Saturday in September, for example) or end (on a sunny day in June four years later) because an internal journey begins long before and continues long after the few years you actually spend on a college campus. The spirit in which you make the trip is essential to its success, so hang on to the hope and the enthusiasm you feel as you look forward to college; the feelings can be an investment with a high yield. One student expresses the thrill this way:

> What an experience! I have learned so much and unlearned even more—a kind of "creative destruction" went on in my mind.... Old stereotypes and preoccupations were shattered; I felt like my head was being split open, emptied, and refilled. With what, I am still trying to discover.

This chapter is about the "old stereotypes and preoccupations" you may carry with you on the journey—your assumptions about college and yourself. It is also about expectations. Some of these notions may allow you to believe in certain myths of college without being critical enough of them. We'll look at that in a moment, but first, as a way of getting at these notions, imagine yourself in the two photographs below.

## **PORTRAITS**

The first is a snapshot for the family album taken by one of your parents on the day you leave home for college. You are standing on the platform of the bus station in your town, looking toward the camera. You are alone, waving to your parents, a small duffel bag at your feet. You are wearing a sweatshirt with the name of your college across the front in four-inch-high letters. Otherwise, you are dressed as you have always dressed at home. What is most striking about the picture is the expression on your face.

You look both terrified and ready for anything. It is a rare combination of looks.

The second picture is in what is called the view book of your college, the booklet used by the admissions office to describe the college to prospective applicants. In this picture, you are standing with another student on the steps of the library, not looking at the camera, talking with a professor. He is dressed in rumpled tweeds and is smoking a pipe. You and the other student are dressed similarly in L.L. Bean sweaters. The college sweatshirt is gone. In a backpack slung over one shoulder you carry what looks like books, and there is a pencil behind your ear. You are talking and gesturing earnestly. Both the professor and the other student seem to be paying close attention to you.

## Myths

If we look closely, we can see that these pictures represent some of the ideas beginning students carry with them as spiritual baggage. We should think about some of these myths concerning college here in this first chapter before we approach the actual experience of college. *Myth* here means something simple: an idea people have, usually received from others and much changed as it is passed along, that claims to describe completely how things are. You should test the myths about college that follow to see which ones you believe and whether some of your myths are different. Also test them against accounts later in this book that claim to be objective and accurate. You probably already have some pieces of some of these accounts in your head, and they may seem to conflict with one another.

Look closely at the pictures. The version of you in the family snapshot is headed for a great unknown full of promise. You are leaving what's familiar way behind; you must take a long-distance bus to get where you are going. You are alone, managing the trip yourself; no parent is in the picture. You are ready to give your allegiance to your college, and you announce boldly where you are going. You travel light. There are no books in sight. You will acquire most of what you will need to live in your new world after you arrive.

In the picture in the view book, you have been at college for a while. You stand with an attitude different from that of the innocent on the station platform—as though you haven't a fear in the world. You have arrived. You talk with the professor as an equal and he has all afternoon for you. His pipe is stoked and his tweeds are warm. You and the other student are carrying textbooks and notebooks, but you don't seem to need to refer to them, although apparently the conversation is intellectual, not about who will win the hockey game tonight. You look as though you are discussing Hamlet's indecision and are about to suggest skipping band practice to go for coffee. You are, all three, members of a company of educated people.

We need a catalog of some of the myths illustrated by the pictures. Like all myths, they are true and false; some of them even come in positive and negative versions. For the moment, just take them in, with all their contradictions. By the time we have finished with this book we will have looked at all of them critically, but as you read now ask yourself what these versions of college include that seems more or less true, and what they leave out that might also be true, more or less.

## FACT OR FICTION?

### The Myth of Guaranteed Success

Is one of the things you say to yourself about college that it is a ticket to success? If so, you might pause and ask what you mean by "success." Perhaps that your college degree, represented by a diploma certifying that you have completed a set of requirements, will give you access to people and opportunities from which you would otherwise be cut off. You will be connected by virtue of that certificate to all the other graduates of your college and to the people they are associated with, and you will be able to depend on that network. You have even heard whispers that if you are "good enough" to get admitted to certain student organizations at certain colleges, you are guaranteed a certain income for life. In newspapers and magazines, you read biographies and profiles of people whose power, prestige, and wealth seem to result directly from the fact that they are college graduates. The four years of college guarantee that your contributions in later life will produce significant rewards.

## The Myth of Intellectual Purity

On the other hand, you may not be thinking about success at all. In college you will be surrounded by smart people. You don't think you're so brainy, but you're tired of being called weird by people at school because you like to read or because you know the answers to questions. At the moment, you're not thinking about what will come after college but only how wonderful it will be to stay up for all-night bull sessions with your friends and roommates, talking about the issues surrounding a woman's legal freedom to have an abortion or trying to settle which of Woody Allen's movies is the best. Everyone at college will have as much enthusiasm as you do for such wonderful talk. Ideas will be treated as though they are important. You will grow intellectually because you will be with other young people who want to grow intellectually. College life will be pure.

Questions: Does one or the other of these strike you as a realistic view? Can you find parts of a more complete view in both versions? Is a balancing or combining of some sort called for?

## The Myth of the Kindly Faculty

The creators and preservers of the intellectual tone of the college are the faculty. Dedicated scholars and devoted teachers of younger people, the faculty are there to work with you, to teach you what they know, and to inspire you to learn what they do not yet know. After all, if the relationship between teacher and student is not at the heart of a college, what is? College instructors will be more skillful than high school teachers, and every class meeting will be an inspiration. You plan to pay close attention, ask good questions, and receive marvelous answers. College teachers have an endless capacity for coffee in the student union or at that little cappuccino place near the campus and are just waiting for invitations.

## The Myth of the Absentee Faculty

You may believe quite otherwise about the faculty, assuming you will probably never really talk with a senior professor. Dedicated scholars, respected professionals in their fields, the faculty are at the college to do their own work on the cutting edge and to let that work trickle down to affect what you learn. You will be taught by graduate students or inexperienced junior faculty members, who won't know much about teaching. You understand that this risk is especially great in large universities, but you believe it is also a problem at small colleges, where the faculty want to be compared favorably with their university colleagues. No professor will ever invite you home for dinner. Every course you take in the first couple of years will have 200 students. The Nobel laureate who is teaching the course will stand the length of a football field away behind a podium. Seminars with six people, including the professor, sitting in the sunshine under a tree, trying to concentrate on Plato while a purple finch sings close by, are a dream.

Questions: Can you figure out how to get either or both of these accounts of faculty members into perspective relative to your hopes? Can you see your way clear to the education you want at the hands of such teachers? Can you state your own goals and say what you want your work with college teachers to accomplish?

## The Myth of the Preppy Edge

People who have been to private schools have a huge advantage over public school graduates once everybody gets to college. Prep school classes are like classes in college, with heavy, long-term reading and writing assignments and vigorous discussion around small tables. Standards for written and quantitative work are high. Social life is sophisticated. With some rare exceptions, public high school graduates don't know much, can't do much, and, though the native ability may be there, have a rough time catching up. To top it off, private school alumni are already on the "inside": They are connected to a network that will guarantee them success in college and afterwards simply by virtue of having graduated from one of these schools.

Questions: If this account is true, what difference might it make in your approach to college and to your fellow students? How might it matter if this account isn't true?

## The Myth of the Golden Age

The college years will be the best years of your life. People who have been to college tell you this. You have heard the claim so often it must be true. So you're looking forward to roommates who will share the most intimate details of their lives with you and will express perfect sympathy in the rare painful times, and to teammates who will be the finest people you have ever known. You will never again feel the same sense of achievement. Your college travels will be the most adventurous, college social gatherings will be the least phony, college romances will be the most passionate. You will accomplish fiscal miracles on no money. You will not catch mononucleosis or need arthroscopic surgery.

Questions: However engaging the stories about the "best years," haven't you heard other sorts of stories? What do you make of the differences among stories? How do you put them together?

## The Myth of Entitlement

You are sure that it will be a miracle if you are admitted to the college you want to attend. You have finally managed to convince yourself that you are smart enough to get in, and you have put together an impressive enough academic and extracurricular record, but you are just not the sort that ever gets admitted to that college. No one in your family has ever gone to college; you and your family have no money; you are from the wrong side of the tracks; 20 years ago the college was single sex and you are a member of the recently recognized gender. They will just never take you.

If they do accept you, they won't mean it, you believe, because of one or more of the items on the list in the previous paragraph. Or perhaps you believe this because you are a member of a minority group, or because you are from a tiny town and high school where nobody has ever gone out of state, or because you are an athlete, or because the only people who really belong there are people whose relatives are alumni.

Perhaps you are a member of just such a family and believe that admission to the college was guaranteed you at birth—and you worry that that is the only reason they will take you. You know for a fact that you could not have done well enough to merit admission in your own right. Certainly volunteering at the hospital near your high school won't count for anything in the face of your failure to make the field hockey team in the ninth grade.

Maybe, in spite of yourself, you want to go to the only college in the country where, if you get in, you will be the sole mistake made by the admission committee that year. They will have missed how mediocre you are, or the computer will have put you on the wrong list.

Or perhaps you will get into your college from the waiting list and everybody else will know that, and you will be forever second rate.

Question: If everybody in college believes one or more of these things, who does feel entitled?

## The Myth of Freedom

More important than anything else is the freedom college life will allow you. You will be on your own. No one will check whether you come in on time at night. No one will nag you about doing your homework. No one will tell you how to spend your money or worry about whether the job you take to earn it is cool. You will be free to make whatever friends you want and to be whichever "new you" seems right at the moment; no one in this new world will have any preconceived ideas about who you are or what you do. Your slate will be cleaner than it has ever been or is ever likely to be again. You are certain about this freedom. After all, colleges practically define themselves in these terms.

In this view, the emphasis is on freedom from interference and limits. It is a romantic but restricted view in which freedom is not particularly creative—or accompanied by responsibilities. Sometimes, as it turns out, freedom can hit pretty hard.

> *The anxieties which exist before matriculation are somewhat extraneous—wonderings about the social life, the difficulty of the academics, and the idea of being away from home, mom and dad. Most students look beyond these queries, believing that college will be enjoyable and relaxing. Regrettably, they are not told of the hardships of independence, the unanswered questions which will arise, or the self-doubt which will pervade their actions. This is not to say that college is not an important—and for many the essential—part of the course of maturation. However, students approach these years of freedom with the wrong attitude. Rather than concentrate on expanding their present selves, freshmen attempt to reconstruct their entire personalities. Tearing apart what they already are, the result of 18 years of life, they try to start again, only to create insecurities and doubts which never existed before. The unsure are jealous of those who seemed to be finished with this rebuilding, having obtained a sense of who they are and where they are going.*

Of all the myths, this myth of freedom can most deeply affect how you look forward to college and how you may behave once you get there. At the same time these notions of freedom are beginning to operate on you, you can feel held back more than ever before. Recognizing this lets us move from the certainties of the myths of college to some of the real uncertainties that people going through this experience almost always feel.

## **CONFUSION**

Your parents and teachers certainly have kept after you, and you will be glad to get out from under, but you also know how much they care about you, how highly they think of you, and what hopes they have for you. So you find yourself in a bind. Can you cut loose while not forgetting how much you owe the people who have supported you as you approached college?

All through school your teachers have made assumptions based on your performance about how good you might be at certain things, and they have sometimes seemed to confuse your apparent talent with your true interests and commitments. Your coach and the director of the annual musical have done the same thing. Your parents, thinking they knew what you were up to in school, have ridden the same bandwagon, acting as though it is unarguable that your future lies in sprinting or stage lighting or linguistics. All their support as you sorted out your ideas about college and the application process seems to have been based on these assumptions that they've made in good faith. They seem to think that since this is what you are good at, this is the sort of person you must be. You have accepted some of what they have said to you during this time when your activities have become more and more focused, but you know some of it is not quite right. You know you will have to work hard to make this clear to them, but you're not so sure you want to, because you don't yet know what you can offer them in place of their certainty. And you're beginning to sense that your ideas about yourself can change radically in the first year of college.

> *I first arrived at college confident of majoring in physics, becoming a superstar athlete in track and field, and finding a perfectly comfortable social atmosphere. I went home in June determined never to take another physics course, ten pounds overweight, out of shape, and convinced that the eastern portion of America was insane and should be sunk in the Atlantic. The list of bad experiences, sleepless nights, calling home in tears to my parents far exceeds the happy memories. The irony is I can't wait to go back in the fall.*

However mistaken your teachers sometimes seem about how your grades and scores represent you or how misguided your coaches appear to be about your talents and your interests, your parents present the biggest dilemma. They want so much for you—and for themselves. They take so much for granted and are so proud of you. You've tried hard not to disappoint them. What if you disappoint them now at this crucial point? The truth about your talents and interests must come out when you get to college—there will be no keeping it under wraps anymore. How hurt will they be? How best to minimize that hurt?

## What You'll Leave Behind

Your parents don't seem to share your enthusiasm about college's promise of freedom, either. You can't tell whether they realize they are going to have to let you go. This is complicated because you're not sure you want them to let go completely—not just yet. You are going very far away. How are you and your folks going to try to bridge the distance? Will you have to call home every week? What will your roommates think of you if you do that? And yet how can you not talk to your parents after all these years of being in the same house? And what if you get homesick like some kid at summer camp? Or what if you and your parents have never been very close? You look forward to leaving home with a certain sense of relief but also with concern that the distance between you may widen, even become unbridgeable. These may be pressing issues for you even if your college is not to be very far away on the map, because it may seem far away for reasons others than geography.

You have a group of close friends in high school. You will be leaving them behind; not many of them are interested in the same colleges you are. What will happen to those friendships? Will new friends completely displace the people to whom you have been so close for so long?

As questions about leaving home begin to take more of your attention, you realize it is hardest to think about leaving the person you have fallen in love with in the past six months. You have no idea how to handle that. If going away to college is to be a test of your relationship, will you both pass? Is it possible, feeling as you do now, that you could fall in love with someone new once you get to college? How will you work that out long-distance?

## Financial Worries

You also find yourself thinking and worrying about money more than you are used to. College costs seem greater than anything you can conceive of or anybody should be expected to come up with. Your family will be asked to pay thousands of dollars you're sure they don't have, although you've never sat down to talk about how much money might be available for college. (Is this something you might begin to do?) Financial aid forms give you a way to begin to organize your thinking. You know already that you are going to have to work every summer, trying to earn as much as possible. You think you will have to work during school, too, maybe as many as 10 to 15 hours a week. Paying for your education is one of the most daunting problems you have ever had to think about, and you are sensitive to the pressures on your parents.

How are you going to make their investment in you pay off? Must every course you sign up for have some practical return? Do you have to study economics, for example, because you've heard it is the only way to be sure you can earn a living? Otherwise, are you going to feel as though you are pouring money down the drain and mortgaging your parents' lives? Given this financial pressure, you may think you need to decide even before you leave home what you are going to do with the rest of your life, settle on a career that will meet the expectations your parents and everybody else seem to have for you, and prove that the investment made in your education has been wise.

You know your parents will have good advice for you—so will experienced family friends, teachers and counselors, and advisers at your college. And you know you will be able to work this out—put other people's expectations in perspective and sort out the financial difficulties. Many people have gone to college before you. They must have had to answer these questions, too. You know some of them have loved their time in college. But still the uncertainty is pretty rough.

During your first year you may ache to go home so you can smell and touch what is familiar. When you finally get there in early June, you may discover that your spiritual compass has swung and you have begun to think about school as though it were home, and home as a place you visit. You admit you were beginning to feel this as early as Thanksgiving, when you discovered that everybody at home had changed. Friends and family weren't so smart and interesting as they had been the summer before you left. Your parents weren't up on the real issues of our time. Nor were they as enthusiastic as you hoped they'd be about the films you liked. They didn't and still don't, now in the summer after your freshman year, understand how you can be critical of your college's investment policies, when just a few months ago you were so desperate to be admitted.

> *I feel very ambivalent about returning home. I love being with my family and friends and I'm looking forward to my summer plans (I'm very excited about my job as resident counselor at a program for academically talented kids), but at the same time college has become my home.*

## Gains and Losses

The cycle of leaving people and places that are comfortable and familiar and arriving in a new world of people and ideas unlike what you have known before may reverse itself by the end of your first year and may cause you to feel unsure of where home is. Not only can't you find a home that feels the way you think it should, you can't even describe what has happened, exactly. Expect this pattern of losses and gains—losing people (or your image of them) and gaining other people, seeming to lose the entire, more or less comfortable world of your past and gaining a whole new world—to repeat itself endlessly during your college years. You will change and grow through these losses and gains. You will make friends with extraordinary people, but people you love may fall sick or even die. You will discover and develop brand new skills, but clear pictures you once had of yourself and others will fade gradually or disintegrate suddenly. One week you will feel betrayed by friends or by the college itself, and the next you will be treated more caringly and honorably by friends or acquaintances than you have ever been treated before. It will be important to maintain some balance and perspective as losses and gains buffet you and to acknowledge the benefit of stretching your comfort zone. Keep your courage up and your wits about you.

> *My freshman year was one of the most difficult adjustments of my life. In high school I spent a semester abroad, and I practically felt more comfortable after leaving home than before, so I didn't expect any trouble adjusting to college. Basically, I did not start to make new friends when I got here, and that exaggerated the difficulty of all the other adjustments I had to make. At times I was so depressed I slept through half the day. I went to the peer counselors one evening and found that very helpful. Eventually I decided to try to take advantage of what was here: socially, extracurricularly, and academically. Simply making that effort has made me much happier.*

> *My father tells this story with a kind of sheepish, playful look in his eye. "Here I am in New York, a kid fresh from a small town in Kansas trying to overcome all the hick stereotypes that I was sure my New York roommate had labeled me with, and I run into a light pole. You know, I was staring straight up at the skyscrapers, not paying attention to where I was going or anything, and bang! I knock into a light pole." It must have been an embarrassing moment for Dad. But, after a year at college in the East, I have come to realize that banging into light poles is a necessary part of life. Adjusting to college is an extremely difficult task anywhere, but I have a feeling it is a little bit tougher than usual for a Kansan like me coming East. The intellectual and social "skyscrapers" here keep one's eyes averted from the light poles that abound. I have to admit that I've banged into a few of them this year, but I'm happy nevertheless.*

*Adjustment* is an awfully mechanical word. In the context of this chapter, though, it means learning to carry the necessary baggage comfortably—sorting through often conflicting, more often misleading, sometimes simply dead wrong assumptions and expectations of college, discarding what you don't need to get to the next stage, hanging on to what you think will turn out to be of some use, loading up again and moving on. It will be necessary to develop a skepticism out of the idealism and the occasional cynicism that have marked your views, to mistrust the too glib and (especially) the too complete, and to remember how important it is to develop your mind and your friendships.

## PORTRAITS, AGAIN

Let's look at the two photographs again. In the snapshot, you are actually listening to your mother, who is out of the frame of the picture, remind you that they will see you at the end of October when you will be home for your sister's wedding. And you know that in the small duffel bag are two books, Strunk and White's basic book on English usage, *The Elements of Style,* and George Gamow's collection of scientific facts and theories, *One, Two, Three, Infinity.* In the picture in the view book, the professor has stopped you and your friend as you are going into the library to ask you how the hour exam you just took for his course went. Those small, concrete details of life make a good deal of difference in your sense of what is going on in each picture, don't they? The details in the pictures make them true to your own life and let you realistically question your myths and assumptions about college. The following chapters will provide you with some of the details of college life and work to help you through this process of evaluation.

*It is remarkable how long men will believe in the bottomlessness of a pond without taking the trouble to sound it.*

(Thoreau)

# 2
# Feeling Like a Small Fish in a Big Pond

Let's take a moment to consider your misgivings about sinking or swimming, getting in over your head, drifting, having to navigate unknown waters, and becoming part of a new school. You are not alone in thinking that when you get to college you may suddenly feel like a very small fish in a very large pond. A couple of graduates of your high school have probably told you to be ready to feel invisible once you get to college, especially if you're going to a big place. You will become a number; no one will know you. You're beginning to wonder about how you will be seen by your teachers and how they will grade you if they don't know you personally. You also worry about how anybody will know you personally and what you will be known for.

Eventually you may decide that you can see your education as a long walk, feet on the ground, rather than as a rude dunking. For now, it's enough to know that things will feel quite different from the way they did in high school, and you don't know how you will like that or what difference it will make. Have you ever faced changes like this before? Did you learn anything useful from that experience for this transition?

## HOW ONE STUDENT CHANGED

A certain high school junior named Anton, a young man of good intellectual ability and middling athletic ability, at least as these were measured at his large suburban high school, determined to go to a very fine, small, liberal arts college for the purposes of making a name for himself as an athlete and of perhaps even becoming a campus politician. In high school, he was a pole vaulter with a low ceiling and lost every student council election he entered, after winning all the time in junior high. His high school class numbered 675. Anton figured he was owed some relief, and a college with a freshman class of 250 was the place to get it. Anton's mother told him she was eager for him to get to college because there he would finally be appreciated for who he really was.

He applied to a fine, small, liberal arts college and also, on the advice of his guidance counselor, to a medium-sized university. Halfway through his senior year in high school Anton decided he was quite serious about architecture, and he realized that the college he'd applied to offered no degree in the field. The medium-sized university not only had an undergraduate architecture major but majors in twice as many fields as the smaller college had. If he decided he didn't want to do architecture after all, he would have a wider range of choice at the university. The size of the university would let him hedge his bets, so Anton opted to go there.

But the freshman class at the university numbered 802. Gone were the ambitions to be an athlete of note and a politician who could win elections. They departed in favor of a late-developing desire to keep possibilities alive. Anton felt he could do this better at the university and he was right—given what he wanted or what he thought he might want to do. As it turned out, he majored in English, played rugby, and won two elections.

As Anton's story points out, the issue that keeps expressing itself in terms of fish and ponds—how will I be known?—is familiar to college students and is not trivial. In high school you know many people (perhaps even all of them) and are well known (perhaps even well thought of). In college you will be a stranger in a strange land. Can you stand anonymity for a while? In high school they may tell you you are an excellent student and an accomplished songwriter. In college you may immediately feel outstripped by everybody else at most things. Can you cope with feeling average? You went to high school with familiar people you probably knew all your life. Are you going to be able to make friends in college, where people will be so different from one another? How do you do that in an unfamiliar place?

On the other hand, after several years in the same school with the same people, you may welcome the strangeness. You may even welcome the challenge of finding new friends. You are nervous but also pleased that you might begin to develop new ways with new friends. You might come to feel the way this student does after several months at college.

> *I am so much a different person since I've been here—not a different person, actually, but more of the person that's always been inside of me has come out because of my experiences here. I went to a high school where conformity*

> *was stressed; here I am free to be as normal or as weird as I feel like being. And the people here are so interesting, so different, so stimulating to be around that it makes you grow. It makes you reach inside and pull out all kinds of things that you want to share with these people.*

This sounds as though it might be a hard, albeit rewarding, situation. And life may be complicated by the comedown to pipsqueak freshman after a year of being at the top of the heap in high school.

## ACHIEVEMENT AND SATISFACTION

However you begin to sort out the challenges of being a small fish in a big pond or, at the very best, a new fish in an established, thriving pond, you will have to figure out what your past achievements, the accomplishments people so admired back home, really mean to you. What do you count as achievement? When you read in the local newspaper of the accomplishments of star athletes or science fair winners, what impresses you about them? What seems shallow? How about your own activities? What counts more for you: making all-league, being elected secretary of the student council, tutoring a seventh grader in math? Is that a question about apples and oranges? Then what value do particular apples and particular oranges have for you? It's worth trying to figure some of this out before you get to college. Once you are there you will have to make up your mind about what will satisfy you—because you won't be able to do everything.

You've been doing some admirable things in the past year or so as a novice environmental biologist. How much of that has been something you really wanted to do, and how much has been simply easy to do because someone else (your scientist mother, perhaps) put opportunities within easy reach? How much of what you have done recently have you done in order to look good to colleges? If someone told you today that you could stop filling out admissions applications and still get into the college of your choice, how many activities would you also stop doing? At the first opportunity will you give up distance running in favor of some other less disciplined and less painful way of life, even though you have won championships in cross-country and 5,000-meter races? Or is running so perfect an activity for you that, even though you have never won a race in high school and have no prospect of being other than a junior-varsity runner in college, you will continue to run with great pleasure? From now on, would you prefer to make your contribution to the community as a wage earner, perhaps working 10 hours a week, rather than as the mainstay of the community service volunteers at school? Is there something you have always wanted to do—study Greek, draw cartoons, work as a retail clerk, join a prayer group, teach a little kid to play the flute, become a brilliant playground basketball player, or learn something about investment strategies—that you can do now because you've decided that what matters is that what you do feels right, not whether you are admired for doing it? How important is it to you, on the other hand, to be well known and well liked for good reason, so that you worry that the ways that brought you recognition in the past will not be available to you once you get to college? Will you want to get yourself appointed to a student-faculty committee? Will you want to join the drama club to see whether the urge you've felt to act is based on any real ability and could lead somewhere?

## Other People's Views

Considered in a certain light, all these questions are the same question, one we've asked earlier and one that's admittedly scary: Have other people's views of you during your high school years matched your own—have they got you right, valuing what you value in yourself and in your work and play? This is a useful question because how you want to make new beginnings may clarify the advantages of either a small or a large college. Which setting will allow you to establish yourself in a new community in the ways you want?

Therefore, a college where everybody knows everything about you might be the right choice. Privacy may be the last thing you care about. You may feel community most strongly in a virtual absence of privacy. On the other hand, a place so small may feel less like a fish pond of any size than like a fish bowl in which everyone is on display for everyone else 24 hours a day. Consider whether you might not like a measure of privacy after all. Keep in mind that privacy, solitude, loneliness, and anonymity are all very different things and need to be thought about differently.

Looking ahead, you may feel that you will want to put up a front for a while to protect yourself until you become familiar with the place and the people there. This may be easier to do at a larger college where people won't press so hard to get to know you right away. There is a danger, though, that you will not be able to take down the front when you are ready to, or people will not notice you have taken it down, or it will be in some other way too late. Whatever it is you are finally ready for may have passed you by. Holding back is something to be wary of.

## EXTRACURRICULAR INVOLVEMENT

People choose their activities for different reasons.

> *It was so strange, I thought, to have to forge an entirely new identity among so many souls who had no idea who or what I was. I sought out activities that I knew I could do reasonably well, so that I could at least put on an outward appearance of competence. I think that the tendency to participate in activities in which you feel comfortable and adept is a general one among people in new situations. Despite adventurous drives to "try the new thing," it seems to me most people (generalizing from my own experience) try to maintain self-worth by gravitating toward fields in which they excel.*

Immediate involvement in some activity or even a couple of activities usually makes sense, even if it means making a pretty serious commitment. There are a couple of reasons to consider this, even if you are tempted to wait until you get your academic feet on the ground. One way to get to know people well, whether your college is large or small, is to join a group with members who share some of your interests and activities to which you believe you have something to contribute. In high school you may not have had to aim at small groups because the place is small or at least familiar enough to be manageable. In college a smallish group will be the place to start. Not surprisingly, many people's closest friends have come from such groups—a team, a study group, a musical group, a theater troupe, a political organization, a publication. One of the easiest ways for people to get to know and like one another is by working side by side on some project they all care about.

Another reason immediate involvement makes sense is that the commitment of time and energy forces you to arrange your schedule and conserve your energy in order to do your course work. Your academic feet will have to plant themselves firmly on the ground as a natural consequence.

So even in a relatively large place it is not only possible but advisable to find a small and manageable setting where you can try out things you care about. And in the course of trying them out, you may get to know some kindred spirits and become known yourself as someone of worth.

## SECOND THOUGHTS

It may help you to believe in yourself in this strange new world if you remember that you have been admitted by a committee whose members have been at their work for a long time and know what they're doing when they decide to offer admission to their college. First of all, they are committed to being fair, which means, in part, admitting people who look as though they can be happy sharing the purposes of the place. Second, they are committed to a set of standards that are as high as possible for the college. So they admit people who can not only do the work demanded by the faculty but do it well. Third, they want their college to grow even better and stronger than it already is, so they admit people who bring talent and personality to the college and who promise to contribute in significant ways. Take confidence from the decision the committee makes about you; there are good reasons for admitting you.

This doesn't mean that you won't have to remind yourself of the wisdom of that committee from time to time during your first year. Very few people get through the year without feeling sure at some point that they are the one mistake the committee made in selecting their class, and everybody else knows it. If your experience is at all like most people's, there will be many setbacks. As this student does, you may remember high school, a little inaccurately, as a place where there was smooth sailing, and you will have to figure out what to do about this apparently new experience:

> *My freshman year has been characterized by setbacks. These setbacks are new to me; in high school I succeeded in virtually everything I attempted, but here things aren't falling into place the way they did in high school. I've become accustomed to life at the top, and making the transition from high school to college has been difficult. My past successes only attest to my potential to do well in the future; they are not in themselves enough to keep me feeling confident and worthwhile. I must create a new tradition of excellence and leave my high school days behind me.*

Consider the times you have felt singled out in high school, perhaps with embarrassment, because you did something well or because someone thought you had done something well. There may even have been times when you have felt your friends resented you because of that special attention. You may have wished then just to be ordinary, no different from anybody else. Perhaps it seemed a mistake to show that you knew the answers to tough questions or that you read the newspaper regularly and liked it. There is some relief in this student's assessment:

> *College was, however, the first time that I felt average. Everyone here (or almost everyone) is extraordinary.*

The early months in college may be a time when you can relish the feeling of being average, of not standing out in any way for a while until you have a chance to decide how you want to stand out.

*We said there warn't no home like a raft, after all. Other places do seem cramped up and smothery, but a raft don't. You feel mighty free and easy and comfortable on a raft.*
(Huck Finn)

*I'm going to leave you now and here's the reason why: I like to sleep with the window open, and you keep the window closed, so goodbye, goodbye, goodbye.*
(Paul Simon)

*Good fences make good neighbours.*
(Robert Frost)

# 3
# *Dormitory Living*

Imagine a glorious day in September. Your freshman year is about to begin. All signs are favorable. The trip to college has been fine; you and your parents are looking forward to seeing the campus again and getting you settled in. You arrive at the threshold of your dormitory suite carrying only your old leather basketball, having left your other baggage in the back of the car. No one else has arrived, so you put your ball on the nearest bed and go off for lunch with your parents. When you return to the room an hour later, you are met at the door by one of your two new roommates who introduces himself and announces that, since he has arrived first, he has taken the large single bedroom with the windows overlooking the quadrangle. You can have the best desk as compensation. This is a hard moment for you since you have always assumed that you and your college roommate would someday open a law office together. The weather turns gray to match your mood. You have enough presence of mind to say that as soon as you have moved your things in from the car you'll be ready to sit down and talk about it, but you really have no idea what to say or do next.

Life with roommates is mostly good fun, but it can also be complicated, sometimes from the first moment. In this chapter you will see some of the complexities as well as some ways of working with them creatively. As you will also see, it will sometimes be tempting to run away from awkward situations in your room, but you would be running away from some of the most valuable experiences of your time in college.

So let's assume that you will be living in a dormitory, that you will have roommates, and that your college takes dormitory life seriously, believing that learning to live with other people ought to be a large part of your education.

## **A ROOM OF YOUR OWN**

You have been looking forward to living in a dorm in part because it will be as close as you have ever been to living independently in the way that you imagine adults living. You will decorate the place, or not, as you please. You will be the host of memorable parties. You will have your own phone and pay your own bills. You will have a refrigerator if you can find a used one cheap and, though you don't look forward to wasting the time, you will do your own laundry and try to keep the place clean. You even find yourself looking forward to some of the small trials you know accompany independent living because you will be suffering through them with roommates with whom you are so well matched that you will be friends all your lives.

The reality of setting up housekeeping in a college dormitory may be slightly different from what you imagine, of course, if no less edifying.

> *All things done for the first time are truly experiments, taken with equal measures of care and excitement. Orientation week was an open lab. Worry finally met reality when I began to test the waters around me. The placement exams, scheduled advising sessions, evening socials, and club meetings were all part of my self-expansion. The handling of these daily affairs and unfamiliar tasks gradually built self-confidence, and these sudden responsibilities I assumed increased my capability. Even doing laundry in the dorm and eating proper meals in the dining hall demanded more thought and judgment than I was accustomed to using at home. Compelled by circumstance to solve problems that others could not solve for me, within the week I had instinctively structured my behavior in accordance with what I had done at home. If my dorm was becoming my home, then I was essentially becoming my parents. In gaining independence I became more dependent on myself to organize my own life, the role my parents had always filled for me. Ironically, they awaited the day when all their children would be college graduates and they would be free of five dependents. Here I realized freedom and responsibility came hand in hand, and how much of both I had unwittingly taken for granted.*

## INDEPENDENT LIVING

Keep in mind that the independence of dorm life is partly artificial. The college dormitory is in certain ways a special, privileged world. You will be able to call on trained resident advisers close by, assistant deans and senior deans at a distance, a custodial staff, and a buildings and grounds crew. Your conduct will be governed most immediately by the rules of the college and subject to the college's administrative and disciplinary scrutiny. As a matter of policy, most colleges will grant you privacy and independence but, at the same time, ask you to be responsible for what goes on in your room. Even though no one will be watching over you quite as closely as your parents probably have, particular structures and rules support the little community of the dorm. So a dormitory is a relatively safe place to try your wings in that sweet, clear air of independence. In fact, the college will insist that you try your wings. You will learn valuable lessons from the mistakes you make, and your mistakes will probably not be so costly as they would be in the "real world."

## ROOMMATES

From the perspective of the summer after freshman year, a student looks back:

> *I had three roommates, who irritated, frustrated, and abraded me all year, and I'm delighted to say that we will all be irritating, frustrating, and abrading one another next year.*

Try to imagine what life with a roommate or two or five might be like, whether you've been put together by a committee or a computer. Roommates almost always have to slow down to take stock of their situation and sometimes even have to halt and come to a meeting of minds. It turns out that rooming well with other people takes work, patience, and a sense of humor, a lot like some other domestic situations that rooming together resembles, whether we like to admit it or not—a marriage or a family, for example. This will be true even if you are experienced at rooming with other people, because your roommates may not be.

Who has what rights in this story? A freshman named Lucas was once assigned to live with a roommate from a town that bordered his. The town line was the only thing the two had in common, but they were intended to live for a year in one room, about 12 feet by 15, furnished with two dressers, two desks and chairs, a bookcase, and a bunk bed. Tyler, the roommate, had a sound system better suited to a domed stadium than to their closet-sized room and liked having people around at all hours. Tyler insisted on playing his music, and every time Lucas came back to the room he found a different group of people there, mostly strangers, but always including a particular young woman. Tyler never introduced him to the group, and Lucas was never quite sure whether they were students at the college or what they were doing in the room all the time. Lucas put up with this for about a month and then gave up on the room and on Tyler. Ever after, he slept in the room when he could, but he did not live there.

## Getting Along

This strategy, adopted by many freshmen since the invention of dormitories, has emotional convenience to recommend it but not much else. You have the right to live peaceably in your assigned room. Another reason the strategy of abandoning ship doesn't make a lot of sense is that so much is to be learned from the people with whom you are assigned to live even if you don't particularly like them. They will be very different from you and from one another. The diversity of college students makes learning to live together both an extraordinary educational opportunity and a necessity for building any sense of community. You have a right in this context to the "home" that your room can become; abandoning ship means that you have given up a place around which you can organize your life, a place that makes it possible to thrive away from home. If you don't speak up and take action in this sort of situation, you collaborate with the people who are chasing you away.

Sometimes the stress is subtle and therefore hard to get a handle on. This student describes one way it can seem impossible to talk about the strain of living together.

> *The roommates I confronted set homesick, insecure little me all aquiver. One declared himself to have advanced standing in biochemistry; one determined to end suffering on the planet during his lifetime, and determined that sociology was the answer; one could argue me out of any view so fast I'd most likely be reduced to tears at my speechlessness; one's arrogance about the superiority of reason to anything else seemed to leave no room for the humanities (I already suspected I'd end up an English major); and a fifth I have not figured out to this day, but he impressed me with a mind so confident I get the willies just thinking about it. How to compete with this bunch? I couldn't. The one I confronted most often was the argumentative one, who was just itching to prove himself at every turn. Already, being 3,000 miles from Los Angeles for the first time ever left me extremely unsure, and having the pants argued off me by this fellow at least twice a day didn't help any. It never occurred to me just not to play along; it wasn't a game—I was fighting for my life.*

In rooms like these, so full of differences and mutual testing, the most important principles to keep in mind—the ideas to organize your thinking and efforts around—will be privacy and tolerance. To keep them in mind and to use them well means managing to stay clear about two notions that can be confounded. It will not always be just your right to privacy and the other person's disregard of that right that is in question. Unlikely as it seems, your own demanding behavior will sometimes test the patience of your roommates. And the ways of your roommates will sometimes demand that you simply believe in yourself and hold steady rather than get angry. Finding this balance in the day-to-day affairs of a room might sometimes mean making explicit, even written, agreements.

Most of the time roommates will be good people. They will distribute food from home. They will make their fair share of pizza runs. They will take some of the same courses you do. They will know differential equations. They will take you to the infirmary when you are sick. They will teach you how to use their computers. They will invite you home for Thanksgiving.

Sometimes they will do all of these things. But even under the best of circumstances, the roommate relationship will take both care and work to preserve.

This freshman describes the rocky course of one year in a room of six.

> *As the year went on, it got a little strained in my room. Our competition never really let up at all; we just got used to it. Only now have we really come to live with each other, and I think each of us knows secretly in his heart that he is better than the other five. Our room is divided into three doubles for the six of us. At the beginning I got put in with the sociologist (I was the last one in and it was the only empty bed)—that was the luckiest thing that ever happened to me. He's the closest friend I've ever had, in spite of the rivalry that pops up every once in a while. The two of us, individually and together, have become closer to the rationalist, and the three of us are rooming together next year. We're clearly the closest friends in the room, and much of the time we are inseparable—and that makes it a little strained with the other three sometimes. At least two of them planned to room with us next year, and when we told them, as we had to, that we were happy as three, it didn't make things any easier. In the middle of February the three of them essentially declared war on the three of us—said we were running the room as if they didn't exist. In a way they were right, and I've tried to minimize that; as the year rolls to a close there's a tendency to forgive and forget—but things won't ever be perfect among the six of us.*

There is virtually no successful rooming arrangement that is not achieved by hard work, yours or someone else's. People come to the job of rooming together with such different conceptions of how they want to live that lots of allowances must be made if you are to survive in one another's company for a year. Some people smoke, though they may be trying not to. Some people like Vivaldi, some the Yankees. Some people simply must keep 190 pounds of pumpable iron under the bed. Some are radicals and some are right-wingers. Some people tag along relentlessly.

Some people find it hard to take a shower with other people in the bathroom. Almost everybody needs private time for phone calls. Some people don't mind if roommates borrow their books or clothes. Some really do mind.

## Ground Rules

The following is a story about what sometimes happens to roommates' most carefully crafted agreements. Becky, Maya, and Charlene live in a suite that has two bedrooms and a common room. Wisely, they decide in September that the common room should be set aside for socializing or relaxed studying together, and the bedrooms should be for serious study and sleeping. The drawback is that two have to double up while the third has a single. So, even more wisely, they agree to a schedule of rotation that will take them through the year, each having the single for approximately three months. In February, Becky, who has had the single since December, refuses to move. Becky claims that privacy is suddenly more important to her than she ever realized, and so she simply has to break the original agreement. Since they are all such good friends and have done so well since September, she knows the others will understand.

What do you do if something like this happens or you realize that you and your roommates care about such different things that you keep getting in one another's way? Hard as it may be, especially in situations in which the problems seem clear, you've got to sit down and talk it out, face to face, start to finish, not in passing or on the run. What is the problem as clearly as you can state it? What are your goals, individual and shared? What reasonable compromises can be made in order to achieve shared goals without sacrificing individual goals? Sometimes there will be an immediate return on your investment of time and energy and the meeting will be enough to restore good feeling. Sometimes things will have gotten so far out of hand that a formal agreement of some sort is the answer. Don't hesitate in this case to write out the terms, remembering how important good humor is. Sometimes neither talk nor simple negotiation will work. At this point, resident advisers (RAs) or residence hall directors, assigned to your dorm by the college for precisely this purpose, can come in and mediate. If you want the rooming group to work, don't hesitate to ask for help.

You may have to do some work and accept outside help even if you don't much care whether the group survives. The college will probably ask you to go an extra mile or two. It will not want you to perceive it as a luxury hotel that would simply move you to a more congenial room at your request. More importantly, it is convinced that good roommates don't have to be great friends. They just have to respect one another and be willing to grant one another some elbowroom and privacy, architectural if possible, but certainly psychological. At a minimum, a good room requires closed doors occasionally and open minds generally. But when one roommate behaves in a way that is simply unacceptable to anther or when the rights of one conflict with the rights of another, the situation will demand serious negotiation and compromise or a willingness to accept mediation and perhaps even binding arbitration. In some extreme situations, both instinct and common sense will tell you immediately that things are ripe for intervention. Again, don't hesitate to ask for help if the conduct of a roommate threatens your academic work, your health, or your safety, or if a roommate is involved in illegal activity.

## **DORMS AS COMMUNITIES**

Just as it is useful to think ahead about what it will be like to have roommates and to share space, time, and belongings in ways you may not have had to before, it is useful to think ahead about making friends beyond the room or suite. This is not a matter of scheduling athletic contests in the hallway or playing music loud enough for the whole town to hear. It is about something usually much quieter. You will, in the normal course, get to know people outside your room, along your corridor, on your floor, and up and down your stairwell or entry. A sense of belonging to something like a neighborhood or even something that genuinely merits the name community (not all groups or collections of individuals do, remember) will naturally arise. Dormmates and resident staff may decide to develop this. Widening your circle of speaking acquaintance and treating others as part of the family are worth the effort, especially if you begin to accept the notion that you can learn from other students. And even if you don't accept the notion, meeting people and being good company can be fun.

The social center isn't always where you'd expect it to be. This student was taken a little bit by surprise.

> *Actually, a bathroom for 16 people isn't such a bad idea after all. Our RA had written to us over the summer, saying that it might seem an inconvenience to have to share a bathroom with so many people, but that we would learn to appreciate it. He was right; many of the best conversations took place in the bathroom. If you want to procrastinate, all you have to do is go into the bathroom under the pretext of filling your watering can or coffeepot or whatever and wait until someone else comes along to talk.*

Stories of dormitories that have become real communities are some of the most vivid in college life. Life will seem quite wonderful when your dorm group packs off to the mountains or the shore, setting aside a day or a weekend from the grind of classes and papers to cement friendships and make rich memories. The formation of study groups can be equally satisfying—people who are taking the same course talking regularly about the material or preparing together for the final exam. If you discover that a member of your group has been raped or mugged, has just been told that he is terminally ill, has heard that her parents' marriage is coming apart in a dramatic and apparently ultimate way, or is depressed or confused for reasons unknown—if anything like that happens, and the members of the group gather around the individual in pain, and sacrifice sleep, class, and study time in order to be with him or with members of his family, it is moving beyond words.

## Boundaries

In some circumstances you may have no choice about working toward community. Establishing general sensitivity about safety and security in a dormitory is an essential common effort. The best way to prevent intrusions into dorms so that there are no thefts or other dangerous incidents is to keep everybody alert to the presence of strangers. This can sometimes lead to a bit of embarrassment if, for example, the president or the dean is asked for identification, but that person will be duly impressed, and the embarrassment will be a small price to pay.

Read the following story about an intrusion to test your judgment about where to draw the line. You and your roommates, Pam and Lorri, are studying one evening in the room, when a young man known vaguely to you appears at your door, evidently very drunk. He walks in and sits down next to Pam, who is typing a paper. He begins to talk to her. Pam is more or less ignoring him, answering in monosyllables and paying attention to her screen. You hear him say twice that he doesn't intend to hurt her and that she shouldn't worry, all he wants to do is talk. You remember that he is a freshman from a neighboring dorm and that you recently saw him behave badly at a party. But you don't worry about the situation at the computer until you see him reach out and turn Pam's face, telling her that he wants her to pay attention. Pam gets up and goes to her room, saying that she is tired and is going to sleep. He moves over to the couch and starts to talk to you. Lorri, you sense, has begun to pay close attention to what is going on.

In this situation the natural response may be to play along and hope the visitor and the situation will disappear. But the risks of playing along are serious, since you don't really know anything about him other than the fact that he is a fellow student. He is behaving in a way that is unacceptable because he is crossing boundaries that should remain inviolate unless there has been an invitation—the threshold of your room and the person of your roommate. He is, by any interpretation, threatening. You must call for help from the RA, the campus police, or other students.

When your dorm bands together for mutual support you all will develop an ethos—beyond that of "party dorm," "jock dorm," or the place where the true sophisticates of the college dwell. A real dormitory community can figure out how to express outrage and take action in response to anonymous graffiti scribbled on someone's message board that shout racism, sexism, antisemitism, or homophobia, for example. Such action in concert is almost always heroic. The situation calls for direct, explicit criticism of people who are at least neighbors with whom you have to live for the rest of the year and at most like members of your own family. But the developing ethos of the community of the dormitory may simply demand action in spite of this very real pressure in the other direction—never, of course, vigilante action, but more like a town meeting.

Participating in and contributing to dormitory life may not come easily to you. It will often be much simpler to hang together with other members of the soccer team, friends from high school, or other staffers on the newspaper—people like yourself. But letting yourself become an active part of the life of a dormitory can stretch you and turn you into a more open, flexible, gregarious person. Consider taking advantage of that precious opportunity.

Many students feel as these two do about dormitory living and learning.

> *I think I lost more sleep by talking until 6 A.M. than I did because of all-night study sessions. This brings up a nice point about knowledge in general. The information learned in courses here will be lost before long—mainly from disuse. But as for knowledge of people and living, this type of learning will last forever. One always needs to interact for some reason or other.*

> *I realized that it's much harder to live with someone and be friends than just to be friends. This does worry me a little for next year, when I'll be rooming with my best friends, but we hope that prior knowledge will aid the transition from friends to friends and roommates.*

*If any undergraduate shall lead an idle and dissipated life, after those in the government of the College shall have taken pains to reform him; or if he shall otherwise offend against those rules and laws of the College, . . . they shall judge it most tending to the reformation of the delinquent that he should, for a time, be taken from the College, and be put under the immediate inspection and instruction of some private gentleman in the country.*
(an ancient college law)

*"But if everybody obeyed that rule," said Alice, who was always ready for a little argument, "and if you only spoke when you were spoken to, and the other person always waited for you to begin, you see nobody would ever say anything, so that—"*
    *"Ridiculous!" cried the Queen.*
(Lewis Carroll)

# 4
# *Living with the Rules*

College rules may be different from what you are used to. In fact, one of the reasons you are looking forward to college may be that you believe certain rules and regulations will disappear from your life. Once you are a college student, for example, you will no longer have to carry a pass when you leave the room in the middle of class as you do in your large high school, and the number of weekends you can be away from campus won't be limited as it was in your boarding school. Your parents will not have to ask that your absences be excused by the attendance office. There will probably be no more petty sanctions, like detention; no more expressions of official mistrust, like having to sign in and out; and no more violations of your privacy, like visitation rules. You find yourself longing for the fresh air of college, yet what about the following complaint?

> *Our RA wouldn't let us play hockey in the halls or do any of the normally goofy things that are supposed to happen in freshman dorms. Perhaps this was a result of people complaining, but I think he personally made people more anxious about exams than they had to be.*

At first glance, there isn't much difference between the rule in your high school that you must have a pass if you go out into the hallway during class and a college dormitory rule that says that you may not play hockey in the halls or turn your stereo up too loud. Such rules seem petty intrusions into the life of a mature person. The high school may have seemed only to be keeping track of you, but the college is insisting that you begin to sharpen your judgment about actions that fail to take into account others in the close campus community. Precisely because college represents freedom from old restrictions, you should start to think about questions of personal responsibility.

Your roommate covers the smoke detector in your suite with plastic wrap because her aerosol hair spray keeps setting off the alarm. A student in your architectural history course slices illustrations out of an art book in the library in order to photocopy them for a paper. You and some of your friends, fancying yourselves real computer jocks, display an obscene message on every terminal screen in the computer center just at the time when an impossible assignment is due in an introductory computer science course of 300 students. Your roommate wants to spend the night in your room with his girlfriend and asks you to get out. You find it is very easy to leave the dining hall after breakfast every day with a half-dozen pieces of fresh fruit stashed in your coat pockets. You know a student who forged her adviser's signature on her study card. Someone on your hallway scrawls racist epithets on the message board outside the door of two black students.

What effects do these actions have in day-to-day college life? In one way or another, to one degree or another, actions like those described show lack of respect for other persons by ignoring their feelings or even disregarding their humanity, jeopardize safety, violate bargains with other students or with the college, and violate standards of honesty.

## WHY RULES?

Of course, your college will have rules. College rules will be quite different from high school rules—in emphasis, especially. In most high schools, the emphasis seems to be on keeping order, while the emphasis in most colleges is on the student's responsibility for making sound decisions in the context of an academic community. College students set as their goal earning the bachelor's degree; college rules ensure that all students travel more or less similar paths to that goal. The rules keep things fair and preserve the value of the objective—the undergraduate degree. To begin to understand how this works, let's look at some of the kinds of rules colleges impose. Since you will be expected to know the rules of your college and take responsibility for the way you conduct yourself under the rules, use this chapter to imagine how you will do that and what challenges there may be to your doing it well. You need to work hard in a new environment to understand the rules, and you may not now see just how much effort will be required.

### Kinds of Rules

One sort of rule prescribes how people should behave toward one another in a campus setting. So there are likely to be rules against noise after a certain hour, tampering with fire safety equipment in the dormitories, and harassment of various kinds.

Another type of rule sets standards of intellectual conduct—prohibiting you from cheating on exams, requiring you to identify sources in research papers, forbidding you to submit the same paper in two or more courses (or, a variant, to submit a paper you wrote in high school for credit in a college course), or requiring you to return library books on time and in good condition.

A third sort of rule governs the way you make choices as you work your way through the curriculum. These are the rules that give structure and value to your degree (granted, there's a difference between your degree and your education). The most obvious example here is the number of courses or credits required. Another example is the requirement that you take a certain number of courses in a certain combination outside of your major and another number within it.

A fourth kind of rule defines the relationship between you and the government of the college. You will be required to enroll in some established, formal way, for example. You may be required to participate in a prescribed meal plan. You will certainly be expected to pay your college bill by a given deadline.

The rules in college act as frames within which you have plenty of room to maneuver, so that you can live your academic life largely as you please, in a way that makes sense to you, given your intentions for your education. All you need to do is recognize the limits and work within them; that's a reasonable expectation on the part of the college administration because you accepted its offer of admission. What we have here is a kind of contract between consenting adults. By this logic you have a right to be treated as an adult, and college officials have a right to expect adult behavior from you in return. These rules, then, define a relationship between you and the college.

## BEING TREATED AS AN ADULT

In school so far, you've been treated mostly as the child of your parents. Adult expectations when you reach college lead us to an idea that is worth dwelling on for a moment because it is crucial in your transition from high school to college. The idea, *in loco parentis,* has an interesting recent history.

Approximately, the Latin means "in place of the parent," and refers to the fact that until the mid-sixties, universities and colleges assumed general parental responsibilities. So in those days students had to check in and out, limit the number of weekends they took away from campus, adhere to rules governing who could have guests of what gender when and where, account for missed classes, not bring automobiles to school, and so on.

In the early seventies, several things began to happen almost at once to change this assumption. College students joined the civil rights movement. The United States became gradually more entangled in the war in Vietnam, and the draft loomed over students. Colleges began to admit more and more students from families, areas of the country, and racial and ethnic groups for which college was new. These changes resulted in a new spirit of skepticism among college students about the value of a liberal arts education and more sweepingly about a college's authority over its students. College governance changed seemingly overnight, as students became more deeply involved in decision making. The notion that the college continued to have some parental responsibility was no longer tolerable.

Now students are responsible for governing their own affairs in areas other than the curriculum, within the sorts of frameworks we've just been talking about. The college provides advice and services in those areas, more or less vigorously, depending on its vision of itself and its mission.

In some areas, the pendulum has swung back a little. Colleges are making and enforcing rules again—concerning alcohol and drug abuse, intolerance and harassment, freedom of expression, and other complex social issues. This is happening in part because students and their parents have asked for it and in part because faculties have simply begun to reassert their authority over the curriculum and over students' conduct.

## LIVING WITHIN THE RULES

Try to imagine yourself operating within the framework of college rules. You may appreciate the guidance, you may feel hemmed in and helpless, or you may want to test the flexibility of the frames by pushing against them. Old hands may say that there isn't a rule in the college that can't be circumvented or bent if you can figure out where to push. You may simply believe that rules are made to be tested and that authority must be questioned.

What's your sense of the issues in the following story? In the second term of his freshman year, Sam gets a job checking out books at the reserve desk of the library. Reserve books are books that faculty members have asked to be placed on special shelves for the exclusive use of students in their courses. The books may be kept for only two hours at a time and may not be taken from the special reserve reading room. Before Sam leaves his job at closing time on Saturday night, he removes from the shelf a book for the economics course he is taking, puts it in his backpack, and leaves, waving to the woman who checks book bags at the exit as he goes, depending on her not to check him since he is a fellow employee and knows the rules. Sure enough, she does not check his bag. Sam knows that no one in the course has asked for the book during his shift, even though there is an exam in the course on Monday afternoon and the book is probably going to be important for the exam. Sam is not working on Sunday. Monday morning Sam's supervisor calls him, asks him whether he has the book and, when he admits it, says she is going to report him to the dean. Tuesday morning Sam is notified by the dean that he must appear before the disciplinary committee to account for his actions.

Do you see why this is a serious violation of the rules of the college? No property has been destroyed. No physical injury has been done anyone. Everything can be put back the way it was. It's not even clear that anyone has been hurt in any way by what Sam has done. Still, someone might have wanted the book, and the reason the faculty wrote the rule in the first place was to protect the access of that person, no matter how many hours had passed without a request for the book. Access to library materials is a cherished right in a college. To violate that right for any reason, especially to gain an edge over other students taking the same exam, is a college crime. In Sam's case, no one asked for the book while he had it out. It doesn't matter. Sam will feel the weight of his violation of community agreement not just in his reflection on his behavior but also in the response of the committee.

## "Owning" an Idea

The rules governing "ownership" of ideas in academic work can seem very complicated, especially if no teacher has ever worked with you on the proper ways to acknowledge the sources you used in writing a paper. It's possible to boil everything down to a couple of rules of thumb that can keep you from getting too tangled up in technical detail before you understand what you are doing. Write so that a stranger reading your essay can identify which material is yours and which comes from a source you have consulted. Before you hand in your work, be sure you understand the rules of the course with respect to your use of the ideas of others. Above all, trust yourself to find original ways to say things.

Here are some of the things students do that are considered violations of the rules respecting the authorship of ideas:

- Submitting a paper to a college instructor that was written in high school, even if it has been heavily revised to take into account the suggestions of the high school teacher;
- Handing in a paper to two courses at the same time or to two courses in different years, without having the express permission of both instructors;
- Using direct quotations without using quotation marks and footnotes;
- Failing to footnote a paraphrase of an idea belonging to someone else;
- Assuming that a footnote at the end of every paragraph will cover whatever material in the paragraph is someone else's language or idea;
- Assuming that citing a source in a bibliography will be sufficient to cover any errors in citation in the body of the essay;
- Thinking that careless note taking excuses you because it explains why you lost track of which material was yours and which came from your sources.

This list is not exhaustive, nor is it a substitute for following the rules in a good manual of style. You will want to ask your instructor which manual is preferred. Our discussion here is meant only to sharpen your image of yourself writing a research paper in college.

The following situation demands that the students involved be especially aware of who owns what ideas. It is 2 A.M. Since supper, Marlene has been working in the terminal room on a set of problems due for her introductory computer course at 10 A.M. She has been stuck for an hour in the same loop in the program she is writing. Frustrated and exhausted, she looks around for help and sees a student she recognizes from the course. Marlene asks Rob if he can tell her how he got past the place where she is stuck. He describes a way out. Marlene tries her hand at inventing a solution that is like Rob's, but finds that only the particular way he has described gets her unstuck. She tries all the variants she can think of but finally convinces herself that Rob's routine is the only solution. Marlene remembers that the course has a rule against students working together, but she is so tired she types in Rob's solution, prints out her problem set, and goes back to the dorm to bed. Three days after handing in the assignment, Marlene gets a call from the instructor, who wants to discuss his suspicions about her work on the problem set. The instructor has caught the resemblance between Marlene's and Rob's work, calls them both in at the same time, and, after hearing their truthful account of what happened in the terminal room that night, decides that he must report them both to the dean.

Could Marlene or Rob have done something different to avoid getting the call and having to face the dean and her committee? Saying that students should be permitted to work together, since collaboration will be demanded of them in later life, is not an answer here, because at the outset the instructor had clearly stated a rule against collaboration. Marlene might have handed in the problem set unfinished, with a note explaining where and how she was stuck. She might have started the assignment earlier so she wouldn't have found herself at an impasse, exhausted and scared. Rob might have refused to talk with her (though that seems pretty unreasonable). She might have written a footnote into the program, crediting Rob with the invention of the algorithm. Not something that occurs to you right away, is it? And yet, that step would have revealed the truth about Marlene's work and might have made disciplinary action inappropriate—though her grade on the assignment might have suffered.

## TESTING THE LIMITS

We should say entirely different things about the rules that govern how a student earns the degree, and those relating to how a student operates in the bureaucratic organization of the college. In the latter areas not only is it permissible to test limits sometimes, but you should feel encouraged to try certain kinds of tests. Inquiries, petitions, and appeals by individuals who want to accomplish particular worthwhile ends keep curricular and bureaucratic rules flexible, fair, and in touch with reality. However, this is not to say that, as a matter of principle, every student who wants to set aside a rule for good reason ought to get what he or she asks for, especially if the result would be unfair to other students or diminish the value of the degree.

The following are examples of situations in which testing is appropriate. You want to take a midlevel course in economics for which the course catalog lists a prerequisite course you have not taken. You think you are prepared even though you have not taken the required course. Do not hesitate to challenge the rule by talking to the instructor and making the argument that you ought to be granted an exception. Another example: In November your family moves to a city that is 500 miles farther from the college than is the town you came from in September. You understand from reading the financial aid literature that you are not qualified for an increase in the travel allowance in your already quite generous aid package. Do not trust your understanding of the rules; visit the financial aid office and talk to the officer who is responsible for your class. One more example: You understand that the rules governing the approval of self-designed majors are strictly enforced by a faculty committee. You would like to design your own major, but after you read the student handbook, you conclude that the rules preclude majoring in psychology and law because there are already courses in the subject in the Psychology Department. Again, do not assume that you have understood the rules correctly. Ask the chairman of the committee for an appointment to discuss what you want to do. Still another example: You are very excited about a paper you are writing. It is a good paper one day before the due date, but you think there is a chance that it can be a superb paper if you have two or three more days to read a couple of articles. Don't assume that you are being unfair to other students who are struggling to meet the deadline if you ask for and get an extension. Ask. The worst that can happen is that your instructor will say no. A last example: The rules of the student accounts office say that if your bills are not paid by a certain date you must leave school. If you are certain that you and your family can meet your obligations in another week or two, go to the office and propose a new schedule of payment. You may find that the director of the office will accept your assurances and allow you to continue to be enrolled while you negotiate a new payment deadline.

This list of examples is not exhaustive either, but you see the point. These are the areas the old hands are usually referring to when they tell you that you can get around almost any rule in the college. It isn't really a question of "getting around" anything. Most of the time there really is some flexibility in response to a reasonable proposal. Even unreasonable proposals will almost always be listened to.

## HIGH JINKS AND LOW

The classic way college students have tested the flexibility of the rules, and the patience of deans, is through pranks. Pranks are high-risk enterprises because their outcomes are not always predictable or even carefully thought about, and because invention and sailing uncharted waters are highly prized among pranksters—indeed they are almost the definition of a prank. Giving advice about pranks may seem paradoxical, but here is some reasonable advice anyway.

Perhaps a series of matched sets of circumstances will say indirectly what needs to be said. (You will be impressed immediately by the childishness of these incidents. College students can't possibly behave this way, can they?) A pitched battle using shaving cream from aerosol cans is something that people can get away with most of the time. They'll have to clean up afterwards and, if there is any damage, pay the cost of repairs. On the other hand, sitting around with your roommates quietly setting the stream of hairspray from an aerosol can aflame so you can enjoy the beauty of it will not be smiled upon and may earn you enforced departure. An anonymous parody of the freshman newsletter that directs the entire class to call the dean at home if they have questions about new and hitherto unpublicized changes in the language requirement is something that deans have learned to be patient with. An anonymous broadside making snide remarks about the sexual orientation of a classmate or teacher will not be tolerated.

As you enter the screwball world of college humor you might apply this test to see whether something you intend as "only a prank" will be taken as a prank: Will the victim think it is funny once he or she understands what is happening? Will the victim understand soon enough not to become frightened or angry? In other words, can you control the course of events sufficiently to ensure the desired outcome? It goes without saying that you must test for the possibility of harm to person or property and the possibility of interfering seriously with someone's education.

In most colleges there are rules against defacing college property. Here is a defacing story where the rule was broken and no disciplinary action was taken. It's a story that makes a dean smile. What is there about this story that makes what happened reasonably OK? One year, in late May, a young woman appeared at the door of the dean's office and asked if she could come in. He said yes. In trooped two more young women, carrying a door. They leaned the door up against his bookshelves with a crash and turned to their speechless dean. "You remember," one of them said, "asking us to keep journals in order to be ready to write you letters at the end of the year?"

"Yes," he replied. "Well," she said, "we don't have time to

write you, but we did keep a detailed journal of our year. It's just that we did it on our bathroom door. So we brought you the door hoping it will provide you with insight into the mentality and experiences of freshmen." The dean looked closely through his bifocals. There on the door, in tiny, meticulous graffiti, was the record of their year, the thrill of their victories and the agony of their defeats. He thanked them, more or less, and they went off to finish preparing for exams. The dean never saw them again, but their door was in his office all summer. He didn't know what to do with it once he had read it top to bottom—it was too heavy for him to move. He called the maintenance crew to ask that it be taken back, painted, and reinstalled, but it took all summer for that to happen. In the intervening months, it was a conversation piece.

In most colleges there is also a rule against interfering with regular or essential operations. Here is a story about just such interference where, again, no disciplinary action was taken. Do you see why?

Opening convocation for freshmen was a formal, some might even have said pompous, affair. A pompous event is never risk-free in a college, however traditional. The associate dean, who was in charge, had arranged to have 2,400 chairs for the students and their parents set up in careful rows in front of the chapel on the day before the event. When the chairs were up he looked on his handiwork and saw that it was good. He departed in confidence. The next morning he went out to survey the scene and found that during the night all of the chairs had been turned around so that they faced away from the platform from which all the convocation speeches would be delivered. Unless he did something fast, the speakers were going to speak to 2,400 backs. The associate dean was not a man to lose control; he sauntered back to his office lost in thought. Standing by the front door of the office was a small group of freshmen with time on their hands. The associate dean knew a windfall when he saw one. "Listen," he said, "how would you like to earn some easy money? In the quadrangle there are some chairs facing the wrong way. Just turn them around." The freshmen asked for top dollar, the associate dean agreed, and the job was done—just in time.

There the matter rested, in spite of the considerable investigatory skill and energy of the associate dean, until three years later, when a certain senior stopped by to ask the dean, the boss of the associate dean, to write him a letter of recommendation for medical school. Apparently apropos of nothing, he said, "Do you remember the business of the chairs in my freshman year?" "Do I ever," the dean said. "I want to confess that it was my idea to turn them around during the night," he said. "Oh?" the dean said. "Yes," he said, "and do you remember the group of freshmen who wrested top dollar out of the associate dean? . . ."

A statute of limitations applied to that case of interference with a regular operation of the college, but even if it hadn't, probably no disciplinary action would have been taken. Too much imagination and humor had gone into the scheme, and too little harm had resulted. The deans weren't interested in calling attention to the way they'd been stung, anyway.

The stories of the bathroom door and the convocation chairs can be contrasted tellingly with the story of the Classics Department wall. Although this story is also funny, it isn't so clear that no harm resulted. It is another story of interfering with a college's regular operations.

Some students were sitting around late one evening; one of them was complaining about being unprepared for the final exam in his Latin course, which he was to take the next morning. Someone in the group, after a long and sympathetic silence, suggested that if the instructor couldn't get into the departmental files the next morning, the exam could not be given, much less taken. The group stole off to a nearby dormitory construction site where they appropriated sufficient cinderblocks and mortar. They stole next to the entrance to the Classics Department office where they built a wall across the doorway, preventing entrance to the office.

The exam was postponed. The roommate had his extra time. The wall made the front page of the college newspaper. But no one in the group had thought about the other students in the course who had timed their preparation carefully and had other exams to get ready for. It was taken for granted that cleverness excused all. It didn't, and doesn't.

## COLLEGE DISCIPLINE

For the moment, then, let's assume you have a sense of what will and will not fly, under typical college rules. Now let's look at the important aspects and provisions of a discipline system that tries such matters in a college.

It isn't easy to generalize about discipline and judicial systems, but in general, high school discipline is "executive" in that it is the responsibility of the principal or head. There may be a committee of faculty or students or both. Most often the principal receives the recommendation of the committee but decides independently about the proper response to a student's misconduct. In college the discipline committee ordinarily makes the decision and has final or almost final authority on the matter. Discipline committees in college may take different shapes, from the student honor boards at military academies and other colleges with honor systems, to joint student-faculty discipline committees, to faculty committees or committees of deans.

Sometimes, of course, college students chafe under the disciplinary structure.

> *Freshmen who are disciplined or put on probation need to be reassured after having made mistakes, not just punished. I am not suggesting more lenient punishment, simply kinder and more sensitive execution. Authority in college can be very intimidating, especially when one is trying to learn and make friends in an entirely new environment.*
>
> *I was really shocked to hear that students are not allowed to represent themselves in front of the discipline committee. This seems highly unfair. Should any student be brought before the committee, the student should have the option of representing himself or allowing someone else to represent him, once informed of the proper procedures. As it is now, the student has no choice but to have his assistant dean represent him. I hope this will be changed in the near future.*

Whatever its particular shape, and whatever you come to think of it, the discipline process in college will be elaborate and careful. The basis of a case is likely to be a presentation the student makes orally or in writing in response to a charge. The purpose of college discipline is to push the student to reflect on what he or she has done, take appropriate responsibility for it, and face the consequences as directly as possible. The hope is that the student will learn something important in the process—even from the punishment—and will both be persuaded not to repeat the offense and feel treated with respect.

Whether or not the student meets with the committee, the dean may ask some hard questions. What, from your point of view, is the most important aspect of this affair? What facts or reflection do you want to add that are not already in your written statement? What's your assessment of your responsibility here? Can you imagine alternatives to what took place? On deliberation, how do you gauge the effect of your actions on others? How do you see what you did in light of the nature of this community and its intellectual and academic purposes?

Like the conversation with the dean, most of the typical sanctions or punishments are meant to clarify the student's sense of purpose as well as his or her status at the college: fines, probation (a period in which the student's membership in the college is in jeopardy), requirement to withdraw for a year or more (accompanied by conditions for readmission, such as six months of paid work and a good reference from an employer), or sanctions that more or less permanently remove the student's name from the rolls of the college.

You can imagine some of the immediate responses to being caught and accused of some misdeed:

- Everyone else was doing it.
- It didn't hurt anybody.
- My RA knew I was doing it and didn't tell me to stop.
- I didn't know there was a rule.
- Where does it say I can't do that?
- It was only a prank.
- I had to get a good grade or my parents would have killed me.
- There wasn't enough time.
- I only broke the rule a little.

- I was only joking.
- I've never broken a rule before.
- I didn't see the point of the rule.
- I didn't think I'd get caught.
- I did it to help my friend.
- I was drunk.

As you would guess, these familiar excuses just won't wash. Something else will have to be said.

Discipline is important to think about now because it proves the rules and because it expresses exactly and forcefully a college's commitment to individual responsibility in a context of shared educational purposes.

*Without those limits we would not have known the possibilities.*
(Stanley Cavell)

*There is no Frigate like a Book*
*To take us Lands away*
(Emily Dickinson)

# 5
# *Reading the Course Catalog and Syllabus*

After standing in line at the registrar's office for 15 minutes, you hand in your study card for the fall term, course titles properly listed, catalog numbers accurate, card signed at the bottom by your adviser. You have just enrolled in your first college courses—four of them. How did you get here? What comes next?

## HAVING TO CHOOSE

The course catalog came in the mail in the late summer. Every course offered in the college was listed, department by department, in this thick book. The requirements were laid out there too; the number of departments and requirements only added to the difficulty of choosing from among all those courses. What a menu! The registrar asked you to make preliminary choices then, during the summer, in order to determine how many students to expect in each course. But you felt as though you were flying blind, making choices without any guidance. It might have been easier if you'd had a better sense of how a college curriculum is organized and how to gauge the difficulty of courses. It seemed to you that it was a lot to ask of somebody who had never been through this before.

As it turned out, before you handed in your card you changed three of the four courses you chose in August, in part because you had two sessions with your adviser during orientation week. You also compared notes with your roommates, one of whom knows two sophomores and a senior who went to his high school. You've also found out that you have three weeks from the first day of classes to drop and add courses. So there is a good deal of flexibility, but it has still been hard to tell whether you were doing the right thing when you picked your courses.

In the first year, and maybe a little bit beyond, you just won't know enough to be able to pick your courses with perfect confidence. To know how a course is right for your purposes means thinking carefully, being in touch with yourself, and knowing what your purposes are. Only you will be able to make the right choices, but even you won't be able to do it right away. No adviser knows enough—not even another student knows enough—to keep you from choosing a course that turns out to be a "mistake," so you will constantly need to ask as many knowledgeable people as possible what they know and what they are doing—and you will have to be willing to stumble.

## THE SHAPE OF THE CURRICULUM

Let's look at some of the possibilities in the curriculum from which you will have to choose four or five courses. There may be 30 to 40 departments and programs in the catalog. The list might run from African Studies and Anthropology to Visual and Environmental Studies and Zoology. Along the way you might find Astronomy, Biochemistry, Economics, Geology, Near East Studies, and Philosophy. The familiar subjects of high school—English, history, biology, physics, chemistry, math, and languages—will almost be lost in this new, rich variety. There will be fields you have never heard of. (History and Philosophy of Science? Mythology and Folklore?)

Some of the departments will offer courses at different levels: introductory, intermediate, and advanced. You can assume that these levels indicate the degree of difficulty. Some courses will be called "surveys," which indicates a broad sweep. Some will look as though they are on very specialized topics, but you might not be able to tell whether they are introductory or advanced. Then there will be lecture courses that sometimes meet in "sections." Some courses will meet only in sections. There may be seminars, tutorials, conference courses, laboratories, and studios. Some courses will require another course as a prerequisite before you can enroll in them. Some courses also might be given in another department under another name. The descriptions might vary; sometimes they will tell you what you think you need to know, sometimes they will tell you almost nothing—or so it will seem.

You do know from reading the material sent to you by the college during the summer that you will have to fulfill certain requirements for the degree. There may be some opportunities for meeting these requirements by "testing out" or for being exempted from them on the basis of high school courses, but the requirements will limit the choices of almost every freshman. Essay writing, foreign language, mathematics or some other form of quantitative reasoning, and distribution or general education (now occasionally called "core") are mandatory at most colleges. You are asked to begin meeting these requirements in your first term. The discussion below is meant to give you a general idea of what those requirements are like. Bear in mind, though, that they vary substantially from college to college.

## BASIC REQUIREMENTS

In your freshman writing course you will write and revise constantly, both in class and on your own, until you have written 25, 35, or even 50 acceptable pages of expository prose. You might not read much, or, if you do, you might not discuss what you have read in ways you may be used to from high school English class. This is not an English course. In class you will be asked to talk about how something you have read is written, and your reading assignments may well include a paper by another student in the class. You may have several individual conferences with your instructor in which you talk about your own papers. Your freshman writing course may be pretty important to you.

> *I am perhaps the biggest fan of the expository writing program. And this attitude does not necessarily stem from my belief that the program revolutionized my writing. I came to college with decent writing skills, and I don't think that the class radically improved them. But I think that putting 15 freshmen together, making them consider and evaluate each other's work, and requiring a research paper from each of them is an extremely valuable concept. One of my favorite people in the college now is someone I met in that course. He and I worked together, fine-tuning each other's writing and getting to know each other better in the process. I was pleasantly surprised by the humility and*

> *respect with which constructive criticism was given and responded to by all the members of the class.*

In order to satisfy the language requirement, you might have to get up early. Numerous introductory language sections will be needed, and many of them will be taught at 9 and 10 A.M. After the first two weeks, classes will probably be conducted almost exclusively in the language being taught. You most likely will meet three days a week, which is standard for courses at the college, but you also may be required to put in a couple of hours at the language lab, listening to tapes and responding to them.

There might be several ways to fulfill the quantitative reasoning requirement. Taking a special course designed for the requirement might be one way, but you might also have the option of using self-study books or attending mini-courses that meet only a half-dozen times. Several of the basic computer science courses or a statistics course also might be considered acceptable routes for getting through the requirement, which is meant to ensure that you can make a computer run a simple program and that you can read and interpret simple data.

The general-education or core requirement demands that you take a certain number of interdisciplinary courses before you graduate. At most colleges that have such a requirement, this will entail choosing from among as many as five groups of courses that are offered not by departments but by faculty committees. The catalog will list these courses in a special section, the introduction to which will claim that their purpose is to provide a common intellectual experience for all graduates of the college. You might wonder when you will ever be able to take a course just because you want to, not because it meets some requirement. On the other hand, you might hear that general-education courses are very popular, often so crowded on the first day that the professor has to run a lottery in order to reduce enrollment to a manageable size. Also, there are variations on this requirement at most colleges. Friends at other colleges where there is no core requirement will tell you they are required to take departmental courses distributed in a certain pattern and number to ensure that students do not become too specialized in their studies.

# KINDS OF CLASSES

In advising sessions during orientation week, you may hear that it is important not only to explore different fields during the first year (although you will have to begin satisfying basic requirements) but also to take courses of different sizes and shapes: courses where there will be a lot of students, courses where there will be few, courses where you will be able to participate in discussion, courses where you will mostly listen. This will allow you to figure out what settings let you do the kind of intellectual and academic work you like and find the most comfortable balance between writing and reading, talking and listening, working out problems on paper or in a lab, and thinking about the large and sweeping or the small and focused. These discoveries may be useful when you choose your major. To help you decide at what level you should enter certain courses, such as language, math, and science, the dean's office might give you interpretations of your high school record, including your scores on standardized tests, and evaluate your scores on placement tests taken during orientation week.

## Lectures

There may be several hundred people in a large lecture course. The only chance for participating in discussion may be a weekly section meeting, which will involve a group of about 20 students led by a graduate student or junior faculty member. In lecture you might sit in a vast hall and listen to the professor talk. Most people will be taking notes, heads bent over the writing arms of chairs bolted to the floor. Some of those bent heads might belong to people who are more or less asleep, depending on the time of day and how entertaining the lecture is. It will be harder to sleep in section, unless you can do it with your eyes open, because you might be called on to contribute at any moment. Sections are meant to be discussions of the material from the lecture and that week's reading.

Watching other people in lecture scribbling earnestly in

notebooks might make you wonder whether you know how to take notes. It's perfectly possible that you won't be very good at it at first because you never had to do it much in high school. Think about how you want to take notes, how you can find the teacher's main ideas while you listen, and how you can begin to understand the organization of the material. Everybody has his or her own way of taking notes. It is also worth considering that note taking can become a substitute for listening, and it might be more important for you to hear what an instructor is saying so you can think about it than it will be to record it on paper. (Here's a story that doesn't sound true but is. An absentminded professor once gave the same lecture twice in his course, on Tuesday and then again on Thursday of the same week. Only one person in the lecture hall realized that it was a repeat performance; everybody else in the course was too busy taking notes to recognize that it was the same stuff from two days earlier.) In other circumstances, the opposite relationship between listening and note taking might be right: Some lectures will be so difficult that the only way to understand them will be to try to write down everything almost verbatim and hope to find the sense later.

## Seminars

Not only are seminars much smaller than lectures, their purposes are also different. If there is any lecturing at all, it will take place at the seminar table, and it usually will establish a context for a particular problem that all the members of the seminar will then discuss. There will probably be assigned reading, but the discussion most likely will focus on presentations by students of work they are doing. Papers written by students might be part of the assigned reading; oral presentations by one or two students each week might start the discussion. It's likely that there won't be an exam because the instructor will know enough about the students' understanding of the material of the course from their papers and presentations. Students will bear a much larger share of the responsibility for progress in a seminar than in a lecture course.

## Tutorial

The most radical form of the tutorial is the one-on-one. The least radical may resemble a very small seminar. The one-on-one tutorial is like the conferences you might have with your freshman writing instructor, except that the tutorial would probably meet more often, would not be connected to a larger class meeting, and would demand more advanced work. In fact, it is unlikely that you will participate in such a course until your upperclass years, when the tutorial will be focused on junior independent work or on a senior thesis. In the radical form, you will meet once a week or so with your tutor to discuss a paper you will have written that responds to texts or to problems posed by texts from a list that you and the tutor might have compiled together. Student and teacher will be jointly responsible for the course of the conversation and the critique of the student's written work, with the greater burden falling on the student.

## Labs

In a laboratory at the introductory or intermediate level, you should imagine yourself assigned to a partner with whom you will collaborate in the investigation of very particular problems, usually requiring counting, precise measurement using unfamiliar instruments, and description using mathematics. The lab problem will be related to the material in the course lectures, and your work on it will be loosely supervised by an instructor who will probably not be the principal lecturer and may, in fact, be a graduate student or a very experienced upperclassman. The lab will start with an introduction to the problem by the instructor and will end many hours later in the write-up you and your partner do, according to specifications, in your lab notebooks. Laboratory problems can be exceedingly challenging and exciting and sometimes will even be the part of a course that makes the most sense.

> *Had my first lab today—the synthesis of a coordination compound of cobalt (III). It only took me three hours*

*instead of four. (I'm not as much of a perfectionist as most of the other kids.) It wasn't half as rough as I had expected. You know, they have about 20 Mettlers in our lab alone? It's a sin the way the kids don't know how to use them properly. I could make good money giving weighing lessons. It's so weird doing labs on my own. There's no one to blame but myself. One good thing about chem is that you don't have to clean your glassware. Little elves come at night and wash it. You get all your glassware before the lab from a room strangely resembling a grocery store. The lectures are still impossible to follow.*

## Studio Courses

The structure of a studio course will be different from that of all the other courses in that you will do the work of the course in a room with other students but no instructor. The instructor will visit you occasionally, making rounds from easel to easel or stand to stand and taking the role of critic, commenting on some aspect of the project you are working on. You will visit other people as well to see what approaches they are taking to the problem of composition or construction posed by the professor, but you will work essentially alone when you return to your place. There usually will be no larger lecture or other plenary session of the course to which the work in studio relates.

## Conference Courses

A course called a *conference* will take different shapes at different colleges, but in its most common form it is a mix of several other kinds of courses. The regular meeting probably will be a rather large seminar that will center on student papers written and submitted during the previous two weeks, say, and placed on reserve at the library. The assignment for that interval will be to read all the papers and a considerable list of books and articles also placed on reserve. Interspersed among the seminar meetings will be an occasional lecture by a course staff member or by an outside expert invited to give a talk prepared especially for the course. The visit may involve a social occasion such as a reception, or a meal with the visitor, where everyone can participate in informal conversation.

You will begin to grasp the college curriculum and discover that it is not just a menulike list in a course catalog, from which you can pick and choose and that produces a more or less elegant, more or less satisfying meal. If you read the descriptions of the courses carefully and ask good questions, the catalog will come to look less like a list and more like a map of an incredibly varied and challenging terrain inviting exploration.

## **GRADES**

If managing work load and schedule is a challenge in college, grades can be a mystery. The authority and responsibility for grading the students in a course belong entirely with the instructor who teaches it, so that the basis of the grades in one course can be quite different from that in another. In some courses, for example, class participation—the quality and frequency of your contributions to discussion—will be a large part of your grade; in others it will not be a consideration. In some courses—a difficult science course, for example—the grades on homework and quizzes will represent exactly the fraction of the work you get correct, while the course grades will be distributed on a curve. The result will be that some people will get A's and some may get D's, regardless of what their percentage grades have been.

Some courses will announce at the outset that the homework will count for only a small proportion of the final grade while the final paper or exam will constitute three-quarters of the grade. Sometimes the syllabus will announce that the worst test grade you earn during the term, before the final exam, will be dropped, and the course grade based on averaging all your other grades, including that on the final. In some courses, an objective basis for the grade will be more difficult for the instructor to establish: the grades will be based on the value the instructor gives to your work.

## What Grades Mean

Grades in courses—this was usually true in high school as well, obviously—are meant to give you some idea of how your work compares to that of others in the course this term and also how your work measures up to that done in the course over the years relative to the expectations of the instructor. Experience with other students' work in the course will be one basis for the instructor's standards; another will be whatever agreement there is among scholars and teachers in the field on what constitutes excellent work. So the meaning of a grade will shift from course to course: A grade in one course may say something different from the same grade in another course. It will not be just the differences in the quality of your own work from course to course, but also the differences in grading policies among courses, that explain the variety in your record.

A grade will tell you something about the quality of your work, but you will very likely learn more from the instructor's comments, which you can use to improve your work in the next course or for the next paper or lab problem. The quality of the comments will vary and will depend on the instructor's commitment to critique and ability to make evaluations that are helpful. If your instructor returns a paper with no marginal comments but a B+ and a "Very good work" on the last page, you may be pleased (unless, of course, your own standards are higher than the instructor's), or you may wonder, Why a B+, why not an A−? What does this combination of grade and comment mean? What could it mean to anybody? So you may not be able to learn all that you want to from an evaluation. Sometimes an instructor will give you more pages of comment on a paper than you wrote in the first place, and then, especially if the commentary is clear and about matters you understand, you may learn a lot from the evaluation process itself—perhaps more than from the effort of writing the paper. Usually your experience will lie somewhere between these extremes, and so you may want to chat with your instructor to understand what the evaluation might suggest about the work you do next.

Sometimes, even if you are not excessively worried about grades, you may decide that you have been evaluated unfairly.

Instructors will not often change grades unless there has been an error in computing them. But sometimes a student can persuade a professor that the professor has missed or misunderstood something, and the professor can instruct the registrar to change the record.

## Types of Grades

A brief word about grading scales. Scales can differ widely from college to college: high honors, honors, pass, fail; 1 through 7, with 1 being high; 1 through 5, with 5 being high; and so forth. Let's assume that your college grades A through F and offers a pass/fail option. You might think about this choice: choosing to be graded on a pass/fail basis because you want to lower the risk involved in genuine exploration of fields about which you know very little or because you want to lighten your work load or avoid facing detailed evaluation. These considerations are especially important early in college, but you should remember that exploration is valuable and that you need as much detailed reading of your work as possible, so you can begin to understand what the standards are and have high expectations of yourself relative to them. A balanced attitude toward grades isn't hard to achieve, depending on your view of your education.

> *I never had to study hard prior to college, and hence I was unprepared for it. My grades didn't please me. They weren't bad—I earned a B average the first and second semesters—but I knew I could and should have done better. I see grades not as stepping stones to graduate school but as a good measure of how much I absorbed from class. Therefore, I regard them as important—but not to an obsessive degree.*

## **EXAMS**

The final examination, at its best, will express the standards of a course quite clearly—sometimes more clearly than you like.

Exams will come in familiar packages—short answer, essay, and the imaginative combinations—but they probably will be different from similar exercises you had in high school in that they may ask you to show your understanding of the material by working on a problem you haven't seen before. Sometimes you will be asked to repeat to the professor some of what he or she has given you through the semester, but almost always you will be asked to go just a little further with the material than you have gone before. You will have to reassemble what you know in the course of tangling with the problem the exam poses (whether mathematical, historical, or literary).

## Studying

Memorizing long lists of items won't do as preparation for most college exams. Nor will simply putting in long hours at your desk rereading the course assignments. To do well, you will have to figure out how to put into your own language the themes and issues the professor has explored, and you will have to understand the perspectives of particular thinkers on those themes and issues. You will want to study actively and critically, taking notes on your notes, getting together in study groups with other people in the course, researching old exams and trying out, on paper, your own answers to questions you invent, trying to anticipate intelligently the questions on the exam. Don't be surprised if studying for a good exam in a tough course takes eight or ten hours. In the end, it's possible that you will learn a good deal from exams.

> *About that test. It wasn't trying to test our memorization capabilities. It said, There's a reason for what you studied this year. Do you realize what we were trying to teach you? Do you know about economics now? Do you understand an intuitive bit about the problems in the world? And I felt, thought, Yes. Yes, I didn't memorize it all, but I do. Yes, I do!*

*Truly speaking, it is not instruction, but provocation, that I can receive from another soul.*
(Emerson)

# 6
# *Taking Courses*

What might it feel like to take on the work of a college course? One student puts it succinctly.

> *I knew that the work would be difficult. My conception of difficult has since been broadened.*

While shopping around a little during the first week of classes, the most useful thing you can do will be to collect the course syllabus, the three- or four-page detailed description of each course the instructor will distribute at the first meeting. These handouts will give you a good sense of the work load of each course, its "rhythm," and its main subtopics. The syllabus will often announce the policies of the course—for example, how much collaboration is permitted, what the final grade will be based on, and whether extensions of the deadlines for papers or homework are possible.

College courses, with certain exceptions like introductory math and language courses, won't have daily homework assignments. The deadlines for submitting work might seem safely in the distant future. There may be only a couple of tests before the final exam. The 15-page paper may not be due until the last week of classes. You may not have to hand in your lab notebook until the day of the exam. There may be a whole novel or 100 pages of some other sort of reading assigned each week, but the syllabus says nothing about being tested on it each week, so apparently you can put that off whenever you need to. How the reading relates to the lectures is clear from the syllabus. It looks as though, if you don't have enough time, you can choose between reading and lecture in any given week without falling too far behind. Some people adopt a policy of putting things off and get away with it. You may resent that if you are struggling to meet deadlines.

> *It is too damn easy to get an extension here, and I know at least five cases where people have handed in papers two to three weeks late and have not been penalized for their disorganization. A one-week extension is the limit. Two to three weeks without penalization is disgusting. It is not fair*

*to the other students to allow these students to take extra weeks to write papers they should have written on time, while the people who met the deadline had to pull two to three all-nighters to get their papers done.*

## ORGANIZING YOUR TIME

It's a procrastinator's sweetest dream and worst nightmare, this world with few deadlines where no teacher will check on you regularly to see that you are caught up.

It might also begin to look as though you will have a good deal of blank space in your daily schedule. High school was organized into six periods a day with six or seven minutes of travel time between classes. Periods when you had no class you probably were assigned to a monitored study hall and were expected to be there. Now on some days you might have no classes, and on others only three. You know you will be going to glee club practice two nights a week, and your job as a monitor in the weight room will keep you occupied two hours every weekday afternoon, but you might already see that there will be long stretches of empty time. What did those people mean when they came home from college at Thanksgiving last year and claimed to be so overworked? Managing this schedule is going to be a breeze.

You can fool yourself easily this way until you add up the number of pages of reading assigned each week or start trying to find terminal time to do the homework in your computer science course. People find many imaginative ways to avoid procrastination's devilish snares, but the simplest and most commonsensical may be simply to block out a weekly work schedule on a piece of graph paper and try to stick to it for a while, tinkering with it here and there, until you don't need to refer to it anymore. (Like a monthly financial budget, this is a kind of time budget.) If you can set aside between three and five hours a day for your academic work, at least at first, you may be able to establish a good pattern that will serve you all through college, especially if you can also find a place to study that becomes your place, where the lighting is good, the distractions nil, and the company of the sort that will go for coffee only once during the long evening, and then for only half an hour. If you need to study late—you may see midnight regularly—will you be able to find a place to work that's in a building open late enough? You may have to figure out how to use an hour here and 45 minutes there during the day, too, something that may not come easily if you have always taken half an hour to arrange your desk before getting down to work. So you will have to make choices even about the smallest details of course work.

> *The courses are structured in such a way as to make it unnecessary to do practically any work until the end of the term, at which point long papers and exams that demand a lot of preparation usually come due. On the other hand, the syllabuses actually assign hundreds of pages of reading every week. You have the choice of killing yourself or doing nothing at all, and not surprisingly, most students end up doing nothing.*

## IMPROVISATION

Before going on to look at expectations and standards in college courses, let's explore three analogies that may turn out to be helpful. Suppose you try out for the high school marching band. The conductor sets you the task of learning how to march (hay foot, straw foot). He will tell you what the rules of band marching are, and will teach you, sometimes terrorizing you, how to perform each step and maneuver while managing a musical instrument: attention, about face, parade rest, forward march, to the rear march, column left, column right, and so forth. You learn, succeed, and are rewarded, the closer you come to obeying the rules exactly. If you master the rules, you may be invited to join the close-order drum-and-bugle drill team. If you don't learn the rules, or if you improvise on them, you are not good at marching, and the conductor will ask you to confine your efforts to the pit band for the annual musical.

Or think of yourself as a piano student. You study for years with a teacher who is an acknowledged master of the craft, until you get to the point where your teacher—and you, for that matter—judge your technique to be perfect. You are not just technically as good as you will get, you are perfect. But you decide to quit playing because you and your teacher recognize that you will never get beyond technical perfection. The passion and the genius—the ability to improvise—are not there.

Or you are a sixth grader whose parents insist that you go to a dancing class that meets every other Saturday night in the basement of the church two blocks away. Over the course of the year, the teachers demonstrate and explain and coach until you have the basic steps down for some old-fashioned moves—the fox trot, the waltz, the tango, the jitterbug, the pony, and the boogaloo. But they also occasionally show you something they call dancing, which bears no resemblance to what you can do. Evidently being good at dancing requires that you obey and disobey (at the same time) the rules that shape the basic steps so that you are improvising.

Each of these little scenarios says something about rules and improvisation that will echo through the discussion that follows about you and college work.

## WRITING

The rules of writing are a case in point. College writing at its best is argument that accounts for other points of view and disagreement. Of course, you will probably write some papers in college in which you do not make arguments: You may give your impressions of a painting in an art museum, you may tell the story of a childhood experience, you may summarize the plot of a short story, or you may define a sonnet. But in doing all of these assignments you will be preparing to make arguments.

Whatever you think of your own writing, your high school teachers may have thought well of it if you showed some mastery of grammar (that is, you know the rules for making sentences) and if you could write several pages when you were asked to. You may also have learned that a good essay has an introductory paragraph, a concluding paragraph that restates what is said in the introduction, and at least three paragraphs in between. And the first and last sentences of each paragraph must link that paragraph to the paragraphs that come before and after, in a certain way. You may never have been asked to state a thesis, frame an argument, muster evidence and draw inferences from it, use sources that both support and oppose your point of view and cite them correctly, and feel free to state a conclusion that says things that are different from but related to your introduction. You may not have been asked to revise a paper twice and hand in the first and second revisions. You may never have been asked to write a paper that is 20 pages long.

You will be asked to do all these things and more in college—and to write correctly. So if you have done any of them in high school you are that much better prepared for college work. If you haven't, just knowing what's in store will help. There are some things you might think about and even work on before you get to college.

Imagine walking into your freshman writing course and being told by the instructor that the subject of the course is the terms "amateur" and "professional." During the semester, you will all be working to discover what those words mean by thinking, talking, and writing about them in their various contexts and relationships. There will be no assigned texts, though you are free to study the two concepts anywhere you can find them—in the newspaper, in magazines devoted to sports, in fiction, in philosophy. Class discussion will focus on what the students write about some assigned topic related to the two terms. There will be times when you will be asked to write only a single sentence and times when you will be asked to write in class, with no preparation. There will be no tests. The course will demand that you think about something from scratch, that you examine the usual ways of thinking about it, that you write convincingly about what you come to believe about it, and that you survive having your arguments struck down by your instructor and your fellow students.

It's not hard to write well in college if you have something to say. If you are observant and even curious, you will be able to put together arguments, which will probably run something like this: There is this state of affairs; this is why it seems important enough to write about; this is how certain other people think it works, or is shaped, or has significance; this is what I think and why I think those other people don't have it quite right; and here is where I pause in my attempt to ask important questions about it, though if I had more time I would move in this new direction. Something like that. Writing an essay turns out to be not nearly so mechanical as it seemed in high school.

So you get ready for college writing by paying attention to the world and what you are reading. Being curious may mean only caring about what you observe, but you must have some curiosity. Then you must practice developing opinions about your observations. Some people keep journals or commonplace books to save up pieces of their experience and to practice making sentences and even paragraphs about them. Your teachers will ask you to write about topics whose complexity forces you to hold several, possibly conflicting ideas in your head at the same time. A large part of your task will be to take a position with enthusiasm and honesty and to try to defeat opposing positions—which will often mean imagining a reader of your paper who is smart, informed, critical, and contrary-minded. Imagine an ideal reader, not necessarily your instructor, because if you write only to your instructor you may be guided only by what you think she "wants."

## **READING**

To write this way you will have to read well. The reading lists in most college courses are heavy, so you may not always be able to do it all. Being selective about your reading for a course or a research project will call for judgment, not random picking and choosing. You might ask your instructor to help you assign priority to items on the reading list. When you read you may want to take some time at the start to figure out the structure and direction of the argument in the book or article by looking at the table of contents and the major headings and by carefully reading the introduction and the conclusion. Working on a research paper, you must go way beyond simply using the library's catalog to guide you to a particular shelf, then using the indexes of randomly chosen books related to your topic to lead you to quotes, and then plugging the quotes into your paper where you can fit them. You may want to develop a reading list with your instructor or a librarian; use a combination of advice from your instructor, tables of contents, and reading around in the books and articles to decide which will reward your attention; and rank them in some order—all this before you read any one item on the list carefully. Reading this way will obviously take time and planning.

## QUANTITATIVE WORK

It's worth taking the effort to anticipate the shape and weight of college writing and reading because most of the courses you take in the humanities and social sciences will make heavy demands. College math and science will present different weighty challenges, in part because the leap from high school math and science is longer—or higher.

In high school you may have concentrated on the algorithms, the routines, of math. The basic activity there is doing problems. College teachers and college texts, moving more rapidly than you may be used to, concentrate on theory, and may leave learning the routines almost entirely to you. With one exception, high school courses will have given you little or no sense of how the routines lead anywhere, so you can't have much sense of the integrity or meaning of math, though you may have some sense of the possible elegance and certainly some sense of the satisfaction in doing it well. The exception is geometry, where it is clear from the start that the math is "about" something—that is, the shapes on the paper in front of you.

The thrill of math and science for you may be the clarity of their content and scientists' ability to distinguish right answers from wrong. Beware! College courses will begin to demand that you understand science as ways of thinking rather than bodies of fact and problems with correct answers. College teachers are more interested in process than in product. The implications of this for your experience of college math are large. Math homework will be solving problems, and math sections and review sessions will be further work at problem solving, especially those assigned problems that people had difficulty with. But lectures may be more about theory; and exams will very likely demand that you go beyond the math you have been doing in the assigned problem sets into areas you have not even visited, to see if you understand what you have been doing. So you may have the experience of getting high scores for your work on problem sets but doing dismally on tests. Memorizing will get you a certain distance, but unless at some point you really understand the material and can explain to your instructor what you are doing, and can understand her explanations of what you are doing wrong, you will not be able to do college-level math.

The math placement test you may take during orientation week is a case in point. If it is well designed, the test will discover what math you can do, not what math you have "had." (In foreign language, too, what you can do at the end of the summer as your freshman year begins should govern your choice of courses; what you have had in high school will probably not be a very good gauge, though it may turn out to be a good foundation.) Accept the distinction between what you have had and what you can do; it's important for your own planning because for the most part you cannot know what math lies around the corner. You must master the basic tools, the basic language, before going on to higher operations.

## A Difference in Approach

A brief comment on the points of view of college teachers is pertinent here. College teachers are different from college students, and not just in what they know. Teachers have different interests, different objectives, sometimes seem almost to speak a different language. University biologists and chemists have chosen not to go to medical school, or even to teach in medical school (just as political scientists have chosen not to go to law school, economists not to go to business school, and so forth). In the main, college students think of themselves as working for degrees that will allow them to go on to something different. (Whether this is the best way to look at college work is a question we discuss from time to time in this book.) They want to amass and absorb information, pass tests, get good grades, earn the degree, and get on about their business. College teachers are trying to find patterns and put information together in new ways; they are fascinated by process and relationship. Information is only what is required to give substance to the relationship of one phenomenon or idea to another.

But before you can begin to explore process and pattern, you will simply have to grind through a mass of important (because basic) information and practice the basic moves.

> *Excerpt from a letter to my mother: Things here are fine. I have decided to really try to crack down on academics now that I'm socially secure. I really would like to do well although sometimes I feel I don't have the mental capacity to understand much of what is going on (namely in chem). That may sound like a cop-out, but I can sit in the library for hours poring over chem books of all kinds and still not be able to grasp some concepts. Rote memory (of derivations for example) is what usually carries me through tests. I have a hard time reasoning hard concepts. Anyway, what it boils down to is no matter how hard I try there are just some things I just don't understand.*

This student will probably get it soon enough, but college science does demand mastering a body of material and then taking an analytic approach to a depth that's a shock to most new students.

Most college teachers love thinking about problems; some are impatient with the details of collecting data and solving problems experimentally. So, as preparation for doing "real" science, instead of being asked to gather every scrap of fact you can find about earthquakes, you might expect to be asked by an instructor to learn something about earthquakes in order to infer everything you can about the ingredients in the "soup" at the earth's core.

You may now be able to understand what is happening when one or the other of these quite ordinary college events occurs: You do badly on a chemistry exam, even though you feel as though you know the material and must have made careless mistakes; or your math instructor keeps making irritating slips when he is solving homework problems for the class at the blackboard and doesn't seem to care. You may have to teach yourself how to move beyond basic rules and formulas. This student is beginning to realize what is being asked of him.

> *Overall, my most satisfying course this year was Chem 14. I came to college with a relatively weak math/science background, although I have always been fascinated by biology. I did not know how to study effectively, thinking I could do well by simply completing the problem sets. College taught me how to learn systematically. After living in the Science Center the first week of finals, I vowed never again to enter reading period feeling like I did not really know the subject. I carried a pretty heavy load this term (chem, math, bio, and freshman writing). I had a test every week as well as papers and lab reports due on the same day as all my math exams. Yet I have done much better in these courses than in chem and math last term.*

## COURSES AS OPPORTUNITIES

Our discussion has kept circling back to the two main challenges college courses will present to you: choosing well in the first place so that individually and together your courses draw you along the path of your own education, and remembering that the concern of a college instructor is more about the way your mind operates on a problem or a set of problems than on whether you find the correct answer every time—though you will also be expected to give the right answer. In each case, looking at courses from the outside, as choices to be made and elements in an education, and from the inside, as opportunities to understand something worth knowing, you are being asked to master the rules and then move beyond them. When this happens for you, it can be exciting and deeply satisfying.

> *My case study was written for a tutorial called "The Economics of Government Regulation." Basically it was a*

*30-page analysis of the economics of surrogate motherhood. My purpose was to analyze the issue and then recommend the optimal means of regulating it. In spite of sifting through hundreds of articles clipped from newspapers, journals, and obscure books and talking about the issue with anyone who would listen, for three months and two weeks I got nowhere. My brain felt clogged with useless and miscellaneous trivia about any and all aspects of surrogate motherhood and the economic/ethical "market" for babies. It was an experience I can remember only dimly and unpleasantly. Never have I spent so much time thinking about an issue and getting almost—no, definitely— nowhere. I despaired at the challenge I faced. Somehow my mind cleared. In the last week before the paper was due, I had written nothing I felt was valid. And suddenly, fantastically, ridiculously, something clicked. It all made sense. I understood the economics behind surrogate motherhood. The academic truth washed over me and overwhelmed me with its ease and rightness; never have I felt such amazing enlightenment. That sense of accomplishment I gained from one paper made college seem phenomenal. I experienced the intellectual excitement and thrill of discovery that people so often mention when talking about college work, which made freshman year, from an academic standpoint, incredible.*

*O Attic shape! Fair attitude! with brede*
*Of marble men and maidens overwrought.*
(Keats)

# 7
# Looking into a College Course

This chapter invites you to look through the eyes of an instructor at the origins of a course, its structure and materials, and the give and take of its classroom sessions. Since other chapters in this book have invited you to look at things from points of view other than your own, this one is not unusual in that regard, but it is different in this respect: It is the instructor's account.

Before we hear the story of the course, let's think about how to listen to it. The heart of a college is the classroom. It's the center around which almost all other college activity takes place. Our exploration of college in imagination would be incomplete and misleading if we did not consider the important details of a college course—especially the sorts of ideas and issues discussed and the level of responsibility taken on by students.

Also, trying to see a course from the instructor's point of view is useful practice. In college, figuring out the purposes and goals of a course and being able to state its major themes and issues are ways you organize your own approach to the material of the course.

This course isn't perfectly representative of college English courses (no actual course is), but since you have taken high school English, you will be able to compare what went on in this course to experiences you have had. For our purposes, we could just as well be talking about a history course. The seminar was an upper-level course, so it was small, the discussion intense and thought provoking. The requirements may seem difficult to you. Most freshman courses won't resemble it much, except for some composition sections and special freshman seminars. But the example will show you some of the differences between courses you have had in high school and courses you will take in college.

## STUDYING FAULKNER

You may be familiar with Faulkner from reading a story or two in high school or even one of his shorter major works—*As I Lay Dying*, for example. But even if you haven't read him, you may have heard from other people how difficult his books are. So you may be interested to hear how college students, most of whom were no more experienced with his stories and novels than you are, took to him, and what sorts of things they were able to discover about his books.

One spring, I began to toy with the idea of a course on Faulkner, whom I'd studied in graduate school. Since graduate school, I had covered some of his books in my classes many times, but I felt as though I had just begun to scratch the surface. In another course that spring, I gave lectures on Mark Twain and Henry James in which I talked about how some of their fiction dramatized the ways artists speak to audiences and the ways they work their raw materials. As I reread almost all of Faulkner after having given those lectures, I realized that one of that author's prime concerns was the struggle all writers go through when they try to tell the truth about anything big and complicated—the South, in Faulkner's case. Once I saw this, I identified some of the questions I'd raise with my students when my course was organized and under way.

The challenges for me would be both the difficulty of the fiction and the particular way I wanted to teach it. Did I believe the work I'd done in graduate school was good enough to build into a course 20 years later? Could I maintain students' interest in a course devoted to one author? There were few such courses in the English department other than those on Chaucer, Shakespeare, and Milton. Would my students overdose? I also wanted to teach this course as though it were a seminar—to see whether undergraduates would be able to maintain the tight focus a seminar demands. I decided to limit enrollment to 15 people and began to think about class meetings that would be organized around papers written by them rather than around lectures delivered by me. Each week's meeting would be led by a student who would present his or her paper to the others, so how far we got with a particular book and whether we said anything satisfactory would depend mostly on the quality of the students' work.

I didn't see this as shrugging off the responsibilities that a teacher should bear, since people learn by doing (especially by teaching) and since I was going to be providing the opportunity for my students to learn in that way. In this case they would have to read carefully and write even more carefully as well as subject themselves as discussion leaders to the scrutiny of their peers. I was pretty sure that, since everyone in the seminar would lead once, group members would keep one another from being too easily satisfied with second-rate work and would be fair and kind in their criticism.

I assembled a syllabus that listed the works I considered important for an undergraduate course in Faulkner, works that showed the range of his art and career. Other teachers might have made other choices for other reasons. My list required that my students read at least one book or collection of stories each week for 14 weeks. All of the major works were included: *The Sound and the Fury, Light in August,* and *Absalom! Absalom!* for example. So were some of the minor works, like *Soldier's Pay, Wild Palms,* and *The Reivers.*

I put together a second list, containing the classic critical and biographical studies of Faulkner, and asked the library to assemble a reserve shelf of those works. This list included such famous scholars as Cleanth Brooks, on Faulkner's mythical county; Joseph Blotner, on his life; Michael Millgate, on the major novels; and Walter Slatoff, on images of frozen motion. I required my students to use at least one of these books in writing their term papers, which were to be expanded versions of the papers they presented to the seminar.

Finally in my list making, I made a list of the important themes in Faulkner's work. I did this so that the students could use the themes as signposts to guide them through the world of the novels and so they could organize their thinking more easily and still have energy left over to challenge the way I talked about the books. The list of themes included the past, the land, family, and (as Faulkner put it) the Negro, as well as money, sex and gender, voice, names and naming, transparency and opacity, skillfulness and incompetence, and images of art and the artist.

## The Ground Rules

I made some rules. Since I wanted students to be serious about attendance and participation, I insisted that anyone having to miss class call me in advance with regrets—as though the commitment to this class were at least as serious as a social commitment. I guessed it might be easier simply to show up than to have to make excuses out loud. This wasn't just a teacher's whim. Attendance was important because each class meeting depended on students' being there to present and to respond. I also asked students to bring a representative or puzzling passage from each week's book, written out, with comments or questions appended. I did this so that they would read carefully, try their hand at writing Faulknerian prose by copying his words, and feel some pressure to ask questions about each book as they read.

The paper presented in class by each student had to be expanded into 20 to 30 pages by the end of the course and be as good a piece of writing as the student could do. At least once, each presenter had to discuss with me approaches to the presentation, and I encouraged students to confer with me again about their plans to turn the presentation into the finished essay. Deadlines were important. The seminar paper could not be late. The term paper would lose a third of a grade for each day it was late. The course grade would be a composite of the grades on both versions of the paper and the quality of the students' contributions to discussion. Improvement would be reflected in the final grade.

I tried to be clear at the outset that the purpose of the course was to explore the fiction, not critics' views of the fiction or Faulkner's life or career or relationships with other writers. I set that limit to encourage students to read the primary material carefully and to write just as carefully as well as to resist the temptation to skim the primary material to get to contexts or frameworks of one kind or another—especially important with Faulkner, where the contexts might be easier to work with than the books alone.

The course was advertised in the catalog as "English 197. Faulkner: Examination of the principal themes and certain formal aspects of selected works. Short paper presented by each student at one class meeting revised and extended to become the term paper." Sixty students applied to take the course. Because there were so many, I had each one fill out an application so I could assemble a group of 15 who had the potential to bring as much to the discussion as they said they wanted to take from it. Students gave varied reasons for wanting to take the course—

because they wanted to read an author they'd heard so much about, because they wanted to explore themes Faulkner shared with other writers with whom they were more familiar, because they were doing independent work (junior essays or senior theses) that involved Faulkner or other authors they understood to be related to him, and even because they were writing fiction (stories or plays) that they thought they could improve by reading Faulkner. Nobody admitted wanting to take the course because there was no final exam. I chose people who had convincing reasons for wanting to be there and who seemed thoughtful. The students who finally enrolled were mostly juniors and seniors. Half were men, half women. Only one was black.

## And the Results

Though they arrived quite serious about the work of the course, the students were also almost always relaxed in one another's company. We met for two hours once a week with a 10-minute stretch at halftime. During the break some people would go off together to get coffee; others would stand around and stretch and talk about what we had done during the first hour. Others simply sat quietly or went out on the front steps to sit in the sun.

A couple of stories will give you an idea of what the class and the people taking it were like. One young man, who turned out to be very funny and relaxed (and who became a schoolteacher right after graduation), was furious with me before the course began for having put him, a senior English major, on the waiting list. He told me that he had put in his time as an English major, suffering through large and required courses, and was damned if he was going to be excluded from this small course whose subject interested him. Eventually, he got in.

Another student, the second or third person to lead a discussion, had left writing her paper until the last moment and so could not bring it to class typed. She brought a photocopy of her longhand version so that a friend who was typing the paper could work from the original. Unfortunately, the friend who made the copy used 8½ × 11 paper to copy the 8½ × 14 original, so the student couldn't tell where one page of her original left off and the next began. Her effort to lead discussion by reading her paper was a disaster. Pages flew all over the room as she became flustered and panicky. I have never seen a group of students more patient and kind in the midst of that sort of disaster.

At another session, I was holding forth at greater length than I usually like, not paying much attention to what was going on around me, when I paused and happened to look down. There on the carpeted floor of our newly renovated classroom was a member of the seminar lying on her stomach, taking notes. There hadn't been a giggle from the class; it seemed like such a natural thing for this young woman to do. She stayed there for the rest of the hour, raising her hand from time to time and making her usual smart contributions, as if she were loafing in front of the fireplace in her own living room.

## Learning and Discovering

What did we discover in the course of the term that was interesting and perhaps even important about Faulkner's books? After all, that was the point. For one thing, we came to understand what Faulkner might have meant when he said that he had tried, during his career, to tell the same story over and over until he got it right. It occurred to us that this story was not just about courage in the face of particular overwhelming southern circumstances. It was also about attempts we all make to get at the heart of something that seems extremely important, and is certainly hard to describe, but might ultimately prove empty or meaningless. We could see Faulkner working this out in the development of his characters and in weird exercises in point of view. The effort took a different shape in each book, but, in fact, Faulkner did seem to be trying something over and over.

Students invented a remarkable variety of paper topics to explore their interests. Not one was something I suggested to a student. One of the books, *Intruder in the Dust,* is a comic detective story about digging up bodies. One student wrote about how the character Chick Mallison's coming gradually to understand the mind of his antagonist, Lucas Beauchamp, is like slowly unearthing a corpse. *The Sound and the Fury* is about relationships among the Compsons, a family gone to seed. A student wrote about the central importance in the book of the sister, Caddy, whom we never really know, at least in the way you might expect finally to come to know a character in a book. Another student wrote about the apparent analogy in *Absalom! Absalom!* between artistic creativity and the protagonist's ambition and design for his estate. Still another student wrote about *The Hamlet* as if it were principally a study of marriage—including a kind of marriage between an idiot and a cow. Another wrote about the rules of hunting and ownership in the story "The Bear."

## Success and Failure

My students took on reading and writing tasks that challenged them intellectually. Sometimes they succeeded at these self-imposed tasks, sometimes they failed. As I've said, the fiction is very difficult, even though there are times when it seems straightforward. The students occasionally admitted being frustrated by the difficulty and the amount of reading I asked them to do. Some of their failures came as the result of trying shortcuts through the world of the stories; they'd seize on ideas that seemed to be true at least some of the time and try to make them true all of the time. One student, for example, insisted on seeing incestuous and violent sexuality in every relationship in *Sartoris*, in spite of my best efforts to discourage her. Other students, out of the same desperation, insisted on reading the books as though they were mathematical equations: One character equals Christ, another, Rational Man; spotted horses were the Forces of Disorder.

Some had problems with their writing. One member of the group, working extremely hard and earnestly, wrote sentences that sounded wonderful but meant almost nothing. He made some progress on this problem during the term so that by the time he handed in his final paper many of his sentences sounded good and also meant something. Another student wrote sentences that not only didn't mean anything but also sounded bad. I couldn't find ways to get him to write correct and carefully argued prose. One of the best students in the course wrote prose that was almost impossible to understand because it was so thick and tangled. With great effort I could see through it, but I failed to help her express her extremely complicated and interesting views in simple, and therefore interesting, prose. These difficulties seemed to be viruses the students might have caught from Faulkner; I hoped that once they left my course their writing would return to normal.

In spite of the difficulty and the frustration, though, these students achieved remarkable insights. Several people came up with quite lovely ideas about the books. One student saw Faulkner's depiction of a character's horse as an empty, horse-shaped space in a world that was otherwise full. This was one version of an idea that Faulkner carried through almost all his fiction—the notion that there was at the center of every situation an emptiness whose shape we can just barely discern, a sort of black hole, magnetically attractive, finally beyond the understanding not just of the characters but of the reader and the author as well. Another student described a narrator as "disappearing into his own words." Another was able to say that "the comic becomes tragic the closer we move to it." Still another saw certain characters as "pushing the world away" or in some fashion "losing" the world, and claimed this was characteristic of much of Faulkner's short fiction. A student asserted that the importance of the flood in "Old Man" is that it "destroys order in a man-made world." The young man who read *The Reivers* said that all the adult males in the book were "little boys in men's clothing."

## Emptiness and Art

We kept coming back to the theme of emptiness because of an image that fascinated Faulkner—the urn described in an ode by the English poet John Keats. Faulkner made us pay attention to the urn by giving it various forms: one character's glass vases, another's idea of femaleness, the tin coffeepot full of IOUs in *Go Down, Moses*. Its relationship to certain characters seemed to express in a more general way the relationship of the artist to his work, and therefore, even more generally, the relationship between any person and his or her work when that work is an effort to give shape and significance to a portion of the world.

Faulkner says explicitly about Keats's urn that it gives form to a tension between motion and standing still (and therefore to the question of how anyone gets anywhere). So we paid careful attention to the shapes the urn takes (implicitly or by analogy) among the other particulars of the stories. The image of the urn expresses something about surface and what happens on a surface and what that, in turn, says about what goes on inside.

Under the pressure the figure of the urn imposed on us, we had to talk about art and the ways works of art are surface and depth, open and closed. Talking about these complicated ideas allowed us to think we understood Faulkner's description of a character "walking" into or out of another character's talk. We also thought we could understand a little better what Faulkner had to say about the efforts of puny man to leave his mark on the wall of oblivion. For Faulkner, art seemed a matter of scratching at a surface again and again, until the artist got the scratching right and began to penetrate into the depths to discover whether anything was there. So the possibility of ultimate emptiness in Faulkner was never very far away from what we were discussing. We interpreted Faulkner as saying that the artist's achievement is not to give up the scratching, the way a tenant farmer in Faulkner's country endures by not giving up his scratching on the land he works.

For the most part, my students were careful to avoid the trap of generalization. No matter how tired they got, they continued to pay attention to this novel or that story and were not eager to summarize Faulkner or his work. We never drew sweeping conclusions about Faulkner and his feelings about the South. Someone did say at one meeting that Faulkner was racist. The resulting argument continued for several meetings. But what seemed to engage my class most were the problems of artistry and authorship. For example, Faulkner didn't seem to be very good at portraying black or female characters. Why was that? In the end, the class felt we never did talk enough about questions like that.

Someone from the seminar wrote the following about it in the published collection of students' course reviews.

*It is said that William Faulkner died of alcoholism. It is certain that anyone who wrestles with his contorted,*

> *outrageous, splendid novels will be tempted toward the same fate. . . . The books—at least at the beginning of the semester—are superb. Many students would rank* The Sound and the Fury *and* Absalom! Absalom! *among the greatest novels they have read. Unfortunately, they are difficult to read, and even harder to make definitive statements about. When you uncover a symbol or unearth a hidden theme, it's very heady. But it's rare that you can tie a neat intellectual bow around Faulkner's books. The reason more critical studies have been written about Faulkner than about anyone else since Shakespeare is that no one can figure out what the hell he's saying. . . . This class can be exhausting, but, like a great buzz, it's a fun way to spend your semester.*

Another student offered a different assessment in a letter to me:

> *I think there are two ways to improve the course: first, shorten the reading list and second, add more structure. It would have been great to know the themes for discussion a week in advance so that the student would be able to look for them in the reading. I would also like to hear more of what you have to say about the readings. Sometimes I felt you were holding back when I really wanted to hear a strong opinion from an authority. . . . I must say that giving my in-class presentation was the most fun I've had academically all year.*

## Questions for You

Remember that this chapter has presented an instructor's view. Each student would have viewed the course differently. Can you imagine yourself taking such a course happily or perhaps taking another course whose subject is more familiar but where you were faced with the same expectations? How might you begin to think about the issues of responsibility and creativity in a college course like this, compared to courses you have taken in high school? This course may seem extreme in asking so much initiative and participation from students. But most college courses demand almost as much of their students—or at least offer opportunities to accomplish as much.

*Whoso loveth instruction loveth knowledge: but he
that hateth reproof is brutish.*
                              (Proverbs 12:1)

# 8
# *Finding Advice and Counsel*

This chapter is about some college enterprises that are often called "services." They are not services in the ordinary sense of the term as it is used to designate the systematic care of a car or the comforts provided by a hotel. They can't be taken for granted. Advising and counseling in college can't instantly make things work right and feel comfortable. In fact, the providers of these services will demand that students work hard and risk discomfort in order to reap particular benefits.

A student's first task may be to struggle to the point where asking for help seems the right thing to do.

> *I reveled in my new freedom too much. Many of the pressures (rules and teachers, for example) and routines that previously motivated me to push myself academically suddenly evaporated. At many times this past year, I felt like I was just floating or drifting through college, a mere dust particle in a whirling cyclone. Aside from my brother—who graduated from here this past year—I felt I had few sources of guidance, support, and, most importantly, inspiration. My RA was a distant figure whom I saw only once a week (and even then just for a few seconds). I went to the reading-strategies course offered by the advising center, but it had little effect.*

Solutions to problems like this don't come promptly, or neatly packaged.

Colleges provide advising and counseling to help students gain perspective on their education. Whether a faculty adviser is describing the academic rules at a first meeting, or a college psychologist is asking painful questions about a student's relationship with parents, or a counselor at the writing center is examining the wording of an assignment with a student who can't get started on a paper, the office where that interaction takes place is supposed to be a stable place where a student can see the outline and direction of his or her education.

To begin to picture counseling and advising in college, you might imagine two different sorts of conversations in which more questions are asked than answered. The advising conversation is a kind of teaching intended to help you discover the inner working of the college. The counseling conversation is a kind of therapy in which you can begin to understand the new feelings you might be experiencing in college. The conversations can complement each other and sometimes even overlap. Both invite you to tell the story of your past (where you have been) and your future (where you want to go). Neither is meant to be easy.

Most of this chapter will be a tour of the kinds of counseling and advising that go on in colleges. You will find that knowing the range of possibilities will be useful in developing realistic expectations of yourself and your college.

## THE NETWORK

From time to time, you may find yourself describing to others difficulties you once imagined being able to handle perfectly well by yourself:

> *This struggle with my roommates began to affect my studies a little, so I went for some help. As the son of a psychiatrist, I've been taught that feeling not quite all right is nothing to be ashamed of. First I approached my RA, who lent me a sympathetic ear, and has continued to do so. When my "freshman funk" didn't go away by the middle of October, I contacted my assistant dean, who was also very helpful. She referred me to a psychiatrist at the health services office.*

For the present, imagine yourself at the center of a network of advisers and counselors. Standing next to you is the adviser assigned to you by the college. Often this person will be a professor or maybe a dean, who will meet with you regularly during the year to see how things are going, to challenge some of your decisions, and to help you keep informed about the college's policies.

## The Advising Center

Let's begin this tour with the advising center—an office, staffed by trained counselors, where you might go once you and your adviser identify particular needs. If you have trouble early on with the intermediate physics course you're taking on the strength of a good high school course, off you go to the center to find a more advanced student selected by the staff of the center to provide tutoring, usually for a small fee. Or you find yourself unable to write the first sentence of the first paper for your introductory literature course, so you sit down with a writing counselor, who is a specially trained junior or senior, to talk about how to unblock and approach your topic. The advising center is also the place to go if you suspect you don't read fast enough to get through the reading lists of your courses or if, even though you read fast enough, you don't read very efficiently and can't decide what is important and what isn't. Or if you have no confidence in your note taking, either during lectures or as you read. Or if you suspect (or know) that you have a learning disability.

## The Counseling Center

You or your friends might find yourselves dealing with more emotional issues. The counseling center will help you deal with these sorts of difficulties. You can expect counselors to treat what you tell them with complete confidentiality. Trusting that respect for your privacy, you may find it easier to say, for example, that you can't concentrate on your work because your parents' marriage is in trouble and they aren't telling you anything. Or if you are completely unmotivated, unable to study for more than a few minutes at a time, this center will be the place to begin to work on that. If you can't talk to your roommates and are having trouble finding friends, a counselor may be able to help you explore the reasons. There may even be psychiatrists on the staff of the counseling center. If, for example, you are finding it almost impossible to get out of bed in the morning, they will be able to talk with you about the symptoms and causes of depression and how to overcome it. Or if you think you or someone close to you has a drug or alcohol problem, they can help with that. The psychiatrist or psychologist is the person to go to with an eating problem (anorexia or bulimia) or to sort out your fears about sexual harassment, rape, or pregnancy.

## Financial Matters

If you need advice and counsel on financial or employment questions, there will be several places to go. Financing a college education can be complicated and scary, especially if you haven't had a lot of experience with such matters. The financial aid office is not just the place that keeps you on pins and needles while your application for aid is being processed. The people who staff the office can help you look at your financial situation in the context of your family's finances and the demands that the next three or four years will place on you and them. So if your circumstances or those of your family change suddenly and you can't tell yet whether the change will have any effect on your financial situation, go to the financial aid office for advice and answers to your questions.

The financial aid office is also where the student employment office is usually located. That's where you can find listings of on- and off-campus jobs, advice about whether a particular job will meet your requirements, advice about how to balance a job with your academic and extracurricular commitments, and the documents required for college work-study eligibility or for withholding part of your salary to ensure that you meet your federal tax obligation.

The student employment office is not simply bureaucracy and paperwork; it is a place where you can have a conversation with an expert about how to make a job fit with all the other things you are trying to accomplish.

## Career Planning

As you begin college, you may not be thinking very specifically about what you'll do after you graduate—which is probably a good thing. But at some point you may decide that the time has come to explore career possibilities; that's when you should visit the career services office. This office is a mine of extraordinary richness, and you should maintain an attitude of exploration and not limit your notion of acceptable careers too early. The staff will administer standardized tests that can gauge your interests. Though most career offices are not in the business of getting jobs for students, they will have lists of recent graduates who are willing to serve as career advisers and even mentors (in the sense of showing you where they work and describing what it's like), summer jobs, internships that allow a student to take a term away from school to test already focused career decisions, and opportunities for study abroad, before and after graduation. The career services office will probably be the place recruiters visit to interview students interested in working for their companies. The office will also supply applications for postgraduate fellowships, show you how to apply to graduate school in arts and sciences or to professional school in medicine, law, or business; coordinate teacher training and placement; and sponsor job fairs and panel discussions. They will tell you (and you should believe them) that, although particular courses are required for admission to medical school, particular majors are not; that you do not have to major in economics to get into business school or in political science to get into law school.

## Spiritual Matters

What if you have been deeply involved in the activities of your church or synagogue at home and decide not to get involved in those activities in college—yet you miss them? Or what if you are approached by a religious group that promises you a loving community if you are willing to commit yourself to them and spend less time with your new friends and roommates? If you are troubled by spiritual questions or want to wonder out loud how a commitment to a religious group can fit with the other commitments you want to make, you might consider turning for advice and counsel to one of your college's denominational chaplains. College chaplains will often have a useful perspective on questions about faith in the context of college.

## Peer Counseling

In the early 1970s, students began to establish their own counseling and advising enterprises because they felt that institutional offices couldn't be trusted to understand the needs of students or to maintain confidentiality. Much of that distrust has dissipated, in part because colleges took students' concerns seriously and remedied many of the problems. But the peer counseling organizations have carried on. New organizations have also sprung up in recent years, because of completely new concerns. The most common peer counseling operation, one that has been taken over by the college, is the dormitory staff of resident advisers. In some cases these jobs are filled by graduate students, but in most colleges that have such programs, RAs are sophomores, juniors, or seniors. They are selected and trained by the college, and usually function to supplement the advising efforts of the faculty, helping other students work out emotional and social problems as well as providing a student's perspective on the important decisions students face.

There are other peer groups everywhere, organized in various ways and often equipped with hotlines. Sometimes they are general drop-in crisis centers. But often they are quite specialized and deal with issues ranging from contraceptive counseling to eating disorders, from sexual harassment and rape to alcohol and drug abuse, from issues of sexual orientation to AIDS education. Personnel at these centers are trained and supervised by staff psychologists or psychiatrists, and are prepared both for confidential conversations with individuals in crisis and for educational outreach programs in the dormitories and at the fraternities and sororities. On some campuses, organizations of minority students provide advice and counseling on such diverse fronts as career planning and majoring in the sciences.

This gives you an idea of the range of efforts in advising and counseling at college. The diversity of services tells you that the range of issues you will confront is much wider than you have been used to. One of your responsibilities is to use these resources well, not just in an emergency or out of a sense of panic—and you'll probably need some guidance on how to do that.

## YOUR ADVISER

This brings us back to your own adviser, who is a faculty member or a seasoned veteran of the college's administrative staff. What is this person's job? What agenda does he or she expect to cover with you?

Practice varies, but what follows is a reasonably representative scenario. Your adviser has been asked by the dean to perform a small number of basic tasks: acquainting you with the rules of the college as they apply to you, assisting you in setting up your plan of study, and following your progress through the year. Your adviser has not been asked to answer all your questions, tell you which alternatives are best for you, or protect you from the consequences of making the "wrong" choice. Advisers are specially trained in various ways of advising, but they also have a great deal of leeway in how they actually carry out the task.

### The Advising Conversation

In a typical advising situation, the following might happen over the course of the year. You and your adviser meet before your fall plan of study is due at the registrar's office to discuss your goals and confirm your choice of courses for that first term. Your choice of courses will reflect whatever basic requirements you need to fulfill in the first year, such as language, math, essay writing, basic computer literacy, and the prerequisites for your potential major.

### Assignments and Tests

Once your fall program is set, you might not see your adviser until you face several midterms or have written a number of papers. Then the two of you might talk about how best to prepare for such exercises, how it feels as you work on papers or take tests, and what you think about your instructors' evaluations of your work. It might be a good time to begin talking with your adviser about what has been going on in your courses—

what you understand them to be about, what challenges they present, how well they seem to be taught, and what teaching styles your instructors have.

## End of Term

As the semester wears on, you might begin to look ahead to the longer papers due at the end of the term and at your preparation for final exams. As exams approach, you might continue to talk to your adviser about them and also about how you feel about going home for the holidays.

## Next Term

After your exams, you may want to start thinking about the spring and what courses you want to take that build, in one way or another, on your experiences in the fall. You might meet at the same intervals, talking (still only in a general way) about what you might major in, given the interests you have developed so far and what you have discovered about your abilities. You may also talk with your adviser about your plans for the summer, how those ideas fit with your emerging educational plan, now that you have had a chance to explore the offerings of the college, and what the next fall term might look like. At any juncture, your adviser will be able to suggest that you make use of one or more of the other resources in the network.

## Disappointment

However ready and willing your adviser may be, you may still feel pretty much on your own.

> *My freshman year was a sort of sink-or-swim test of perseverance. So far as support structures go, I feel like asking, "What support structures?" I'm told by my roommate, though, that not all freshman advisers were as difficult to get in touch with as mine (I didn't know who he*

> was when it came time to have my plan of study signed for next year), and I know from friends living in other dorms that not all RAs were out of town as often as mine. I must say that everyone I asked for advice was friendly enough, if not altogether helpful. I discovered the writing center in the fall and found the people there very helpful. Perhaps the college experience is meant to make one fully independent, but handing freshmen a thick course catalog without advice is like giving a drowning man the plans to build a lifeboat. How about tossing him a life preserver?

So it is possible that you won't talk with your adviser much or that you will see him or her only to get your course card signed each term. This might happen for a number of reasons. Some advisers are almost impossible to reach. Others feel that all decisions, choices, and plans are entirely a student's business and responsibility and that only if a student has a crisis or the dean requests that an adviser discuss some matter with a student—an unsatisfactory grade, for example—should an adviser interfere at all. You might even share this view. You also might be uncertain about how to approach an adviser and might therefore hold back. Or you might not see what use an adviser could be. Or your adviser might be bad at advising, because of shyness or busyness or irresponsibility. And advisers often have their own philosophies; a perfectly effective adviser might believe that it is an adviser's responsibility to phase himself or herself out of a job as soon as possible so the student can take over and be self-sufficient. So your experience is likely to seem mixed:

> I found advisers to be there when I needed them, but rarely did people go out of their way to offer advice or any sort of support. My RA seemed unfamiliar with the system and fairly indifferent to those of us on the top floor. My assistant dean, on the other hand, was accessible, interested, and completely knowledgeable about all kinds of academic and administrative matters. But when the time came to choose a concentration, there simply wasn't any staff member I felt comfortable asking for advice. I know several of my roommates felt similarly abandoned and ended up making very arbitrary choices.

No matter what a student or adviser thinks about the purpose or value of advising, a large part of the initiative lies with the student. In this relationship, as in so many other settings in college, you will have to think through what you want and why, and then set out to accomplish it. Even if you don't want any advice, you should be clear why, and clear about what you will be gaining and losing as a result.

If you do want advice, you should talk with your adviser about what you can both expect from the experience. You might even ask if you can meet, for example, every three weeks all year. Your adviser may not agree to provide you with the inside scoop on courses and instructors, but he or she will work with you on questions that you might pose to an instructor or to yourself as you study the syllabus at the first class meeting. The two of you might agree that he or she will refer you to other offices and individuals as often as possible, so that you can begin to learn the lay of the land and begin to figure out how and where to find answers on your own. And you might agree that for a while, as you begin your search, you will come back with what you have found out and get his or her reaction.

## WHAT ARE REASONABLE EXPECTATIONS?

These agreements and understandings are just some of the informal but important contracts you will make in the early weeks of college—like the contracts with your roommates, your instructors, your family, and the college itself. Most of these bargains will be unstated, but they will be a very important part of your process of identifying reasonable expectations.

What sorts of questions, issues, and situations might be appropriate to bring to the advising table? Conversations can begin in any of the following ways and then some.

- "I just got a D− on my first chem test. I've never had a grade that low in my life. I don't know what my instructor wants. How do I drop the course?"
- "This place is not for me. I am going to transfer. It is too intellectual/not intellectual enough/too competitive/not com-

petitive enough. Not enough good writing goes on here. My family persuaded me to come; it was never really my choice."
- "I'm so homesick I could die."
- "I've got this great paper topic. Where can I get more information?"
- "My teacher thinks I cheated on my take-home midterm in Spanish."
- "My instructor keeps asking me to go for coffee. It feels like he is asking me out."
- "Look at what I found taped to my door this morning."
- "Where should I take my parents to dinner on Parents' Weekend?"
- "How do I get credit for doing more work on my high school biology project on the ecology of a pond?"
- "I don't know what my roommate's problem is, but we just don't get along. I want to move."
- "My parents called last night to tell me they are splitting up. Who do I talk to about getting more financial aid?"
- "I've been placed in a math course that's too easy. I've already had all that stuff in high school; I just made some careless mistakes on the placement test."
- "I came here to be a physics major, but I don't like it. It isn't at all what I thought it would be."
- "My English teacher says the figure with the face painted black on one side and white on the other in 'My Kinsman, Major Molyneux' represents death. I have no idea how she gets that out of the story."

Be prepared for questions in return. In talking with a good adviser, you will not get an immediate or simple solution for the problem you present. Your adviser will ask you: How does that make you feel? Have you talked with your instructor? Have you confronted your roommate? Have you thought about visiting the counseling center? Why? What do you want to do? Have you been here long enough to be sure? Have you thought about this sort of first step? What steps might follow the first one? What are your interests in this situation? Have you talked with your parents? Why did you come here with that in mind? Why did you come here at all and with what particular hopes and dreams?

A good adviser will ask questions because any real solution is going to require your participation. This is your education, remember, so the job of repairing it or redirecting it is yours, as well.

In some intensely personal situations in which confidentiality is essential, you may wonder if you can share your problem with an adviser and trust that it will not be spread all over the college. This will often be a concern if the problem involves misconduct on the part of another student or if you think that by telling a story you may be running the risk of disciplinary action yourself. There is no simple solution to this dilemma. Colleges generally ask advisers not to promise complete confidentiality to keep the adviser from being boxed into a situation that makes it impossible to help. The adviser's responsibility may require taking an active part in solving the problem or reporting some part of what you've said because of its impact on broader college concerns. This will certainly be true in cases in which students seem to pose a danger to themselves or to others.

Be prepared to ask some questions yourself to find out what you can and can't expect from your adviser. And remember that there are professionals at the college who are bound to keep your confidences by strict rules of professional ethics—doctors, for example, and members of the clergy. So when confidentiality and helpful action threaten to conflict, the best way to proceed may be to think carefully about what you really want to accomplish and then go to your adviser ready to discuss both the matter at hand and the difficulty with confidentiality. In general, advisers can be relied on or they wouldn't have been invited to take such positions of trust.

## ADVICE ON STUDY SKILLS AND HABITS

Most questions you ask of your adviser will not be so intimate, of course. An area of advising we haven't touched on is that of study skills. Where do you study? Is it quiet, well lighted, and comfortable? How much time do you set aside for study each day, and how do you decide each day what to do? Are you a good note taker? Do you take notes differently during lectures or discussions than you do as you read? How do you select what you note down? Can you sometimes stop taking notes entirely and just pay attention without worrying whether you will remember exactly how the instructor said something or whether it will be on the exam? And how do you prepare for exams? How do you figure out what the important issues will be? How do you decide whether an efficient mode of preparation would be to pose and answer questions for yourself ahead of time? Do you have a timetable for studying for exams that will let you give the most time to the course that requires it? How do you go about writing a research paper? How do you find the best sources? How do you use references so they support what you are doing and don't take over? How do you cite sources properly? How do you frame a thesis? How do you infer from evidence? How do you argue honestly and persuasively and for whom?

All of these questions may be perfectly good topics for a session with your adviser, depending on what you've agreed will be useful for you to talk about together. So such conversations can drift from topic to topic, ranging from how you underline when you read to how you want to live in the college community.

## INFORMAL ADVICE

One final note: More often than advisers like to admit, a student will find the best advice in passing or by accident. A teacher will stop you as you are going into the college bookstore and enthusiastically recommend that you read the first three chapters of a new paperback before you write the paper due in her course. Or another student will tell you enough about how to rework a paper on *Huckleberry Finn* or how to figure out something about Abraham Lincoln that you will suddenly know how you want to write papers or prepare for exams from now on. A coach will say something wise about how to set your priorities or about the nature of self-discipline so that your life in college is changed in some small but crucial way. Or an alum will tell you a story about college life long past that will guide you in the way you live.

Much (and maybe most) good advice will come from outside the established offices and networks. Listen for it carefully, because often it won't sound like advice at all.

In the end, you may come to share these students' view that, even with the best advising, you will make some bad choices and learn from them on your own.

> *Academically, I made some mistakes in selecting courses and I also made some better choices. In both instances, there was probably nothing an adviser could have done to change my mind. And though I made those mistakes, I still believe that it is good for freshmen to make up their own minds based on what they want to do and not on hearsay from upperclassmen, wise as the latter may be. I, however, had much help in choosing my concentration, something I could not have done without some type of feedback from others.*

> *I was not satisfied with my course picks this year. Since I was an inexperienced freshman, my course selection was largely a stab-in-the-dark operation. And this is not to fault my adviser; it's not that she didn't know my wants—I didn't know them. On the other hand, by the end of the year, picking a concentration was not difficult, and I look forward to next year.*

*I cannot overestimate my debt to that man. I was in awe of his precision and his daring. His speech was elliptical, inclining toward the runic, but his lectures were legendary . . . and once an hour he would come awake as from a private reverie with a dazzling penetration of text or motive. To have him as a weekly presence in my life, to meet with him one-to-one every week for two years, was everything.*
(Geoffrey Wolff)

*O body swayed to music, O brightening glance,
How can we know the dancer from the dance?*
(Yeats)

# 9
# *Regarding the Faculty*

Professor Speedwash can discuss philosopher Immanuel Kant's categorical imperative—actually discuss it, not just lecture on it—with the 600 people in her philosophy course. Young Mr. Qwigg (you don't know why nobody calls him Professor), reported to be fresh out of graduate school, has taken over Professor Broadloom's famous course in critical theory because Broadloom is ill. Qwigg delivers brilliant lectures, which he confesses publicly are written the night before each meeting. In history, Professor Netherland is driving you slowly mad because he sits at the head of the seminar table and says nothing, apparently believing that the responsibility for figuring out how to start a discussion and keep it going belongs to the students. Professor Gibbet is paralyzingly boring and does nothing but read aloud from the psychology textbook that she wrote. Nemo, your section leader in calculus, doesn't seem to speak English, but you can't hear him anyway since he never turns away from the board.

These are the sorts of impressions and judgments you might offer in September, after you've been going to class for about three weeks, when your adviser asks you to tell her about your instructors. At the end of the year, in May, the dean asks you to write him a letter in which, among other things, you might comment on your instructors. At that point, Speedwash seems to you more a show-off than anything else. Compared to your spring-term Shakespeare professor, Qwigg seems even more impressive. Netherland's unbearable silences have taught you how to organize your thoughts for discussion. The mere thought of Gibbet's wasting your tuition still makes you angry. You've learned calculus by doing extra problems and joining a study group. As you gather experience, you see some of your teachers in new ways. And sometimes, looking back on a course allows you to understand what a professor was getting at that you didn't understand at the time.

Who are these people? How did they get here? And how do they get away with being so eccentric? It isn't just your own teachers. You hear that Professor Pollifax's chemistry demonstrations have called out the fire department on occasion. Argyll, who teaches modern poetry, doesn't stand at a podium but sits at a table with her green book bag and a glass of water. She digs two or three books out of the bag as she needs them, rarely looks up from the table, speaks in a voice that is almost impossible to hear, and is absolutely awe inspiring.

## JUDGING YOUR TEACHERS

From the start, discussions with your classmates will call for your opinions about faculty members. You will develop opinions quickly because you will react strongly to your teachers' demands and styles. Over hot-fudge sundaes in the student center, the conversation will be about some professor's latest performance in lecture or about a topic or assignment that has been exquisite torture. Students trying to decide what courses to take next term will ask you what you think of Sahb-Turbot in Comp Lit, Keyhole in Math, or Dohrmann in Soviet studies. Toward the end of each term, you may be asked to complete a questionnaire evaluating each class you took. So for lots of reasons, you'll begin to develop notions about what good college teaching is.

> *Perhaps a bit more personableness would help; for example, I was a bit insulted by the lack of teaching ability exhibited by the section leaders of the mainly freshman, introductory (therefore required for further study), science and English courses. (Look at how poorly I am punctuating!) Perhaps a required teacher-education course would help—no, I'm not suggesting this for the high-powered, big-shot professors, just for the section leaders who always mean well but just don't know how to teach!*
>
> *The instructor was an unbearably pompous man who tried to convince his class that he was a scholar in literally every field. He gave utterly ludicrous assignments that only took time away from other, meaningful courses.*
>
> *The professors were really wonderful. I made time to meet with all my professors and teaching fellows, and they all turned out to be very helpful. My favorite class this year was biochemistry. I was totally impressed with the*

> *organization of the course, the materials being taught, and the two professors. It was an intense class, but I simply loved it. I really didn't like my math class. The professor didn't seem to care much about the students, and he just cannot explain things in a logical manner. I made a lot of appointments to ask him for help, but few of them were actually very helpful.*

## A Professor's Profession

F. Scott Fitzgerald said that reserving judgment is a matter of infinite hope; but even in your freshman year, even in that time of hope, you will not be able to reserve judgment about the faculty easily because you will be constantly asked for your opinion. Ultimately, these opinions you're forming will help you to understand what college teaching and learning are supposed to be and answer the question "who are these professor-types and how did they get this way?"

The basic context you are in hasn't changed; you are still just going to school. It's what you've been doing all your life. But the faculty's context is their profession and their "own work," requiring scholarly research and writing, which is not the case in many high schools. Teaching is only part of what professors do. You will begin to understand that in some important ways you and the faculty are at the college for different reasons. Consequently, you may feel as though nobody is taking care of you academically and intellectually.

> *It's difficult to generalize, but on the whole, I felt a tremendous void so far as the teacher figure was concerned. Although this feeling might be attributed to the transition from being "babysat" by high school teachers to independent university learning, I'm not convinced that this is the case. To me, there seemed to be a lot of people lecturing, a lot of people doing research, a lot of people writing books, and a lot of people putting themselves through grad school who were involved with my courses in one way or another . . . but where was the teacher? I did take advantage of office*

*hours for my courses, but even there, on several occasions, the professors showed no sign of recognizing me.*

When you first get to college, especially in the glow and excitement of orientation week and the first weeks of classes, you may possibly and euphorically feel as though you and your teachers are collaborating on the grand project of educating you. After your first midterms, you may suddenly realize that you and they inhabit different planets and are working at diametrically crossed purposes. They do not seem to care how abysmally ignorant you are or even to know of your existence. Later, after the shock of those first exams has passed, you may still wonder how much the faculty cares about students. Why aren't you getting more comments on your papers and homework problems? Why do faculty members have so few office hours each week? Why don't your teachers know your name? And why didn't more members of the faculty accept the invitation of the race relations committee, of which you've just become a member, to attend a lecture by a professor visiting from another college? Don't they care about the really important issues?

On the other hand, the leader of your freshman seminar will invite the class to dinner in her home, where you will meet her husband and children. The instructor of your American literature section is at every women's basketball game. And you hear from your roommate who has just made the staff of the newspaper that their faculty adviser has set up a seminar for the staff on ethics in journalism and freedom of the press. The faculty is such a mixed bag. Where are their loyalties?

## **HOW A FACULTY IS ORGANIZED**

Every member of the faculty is first of all a member of a department (or division or program). Depending on the size and structure of the faculty, the department may claim the teacher's first loyalty. The department's expectations of scholarship may compete with those of students and the demands of teaching for an instructor's time. This is where a faculty member's colleagues are, the other people at the college who are doing research and scholarly work in the same field. The professor probably feels that only colleagues within the department understand enough about the work he or she is doing to discuss it. The department recommended appointment to the dean of the faculty or the president of the college in the first place. The department will conduct a peer review of her teaching. The department will recommend tenure.

The faculty at most colleges is organized into departments (Mathematics, Near East Studies, Government, Physics, Religion) because they are corporate guardians of scholarship and teaching in several disciplines. This means that faculty members have to sort themselves out along lines of expertise in order to be able to form their collective judgment about programs and standards. As a consequence of this delegation of authority, academic departments are highly autonomous, so most sweeping educational reform—and, in fact, most decisions about any of the rules governing the programs and progress of students—can come only after careful consultation and negotiation within departments. Another consequence of the importance of departments in the organization of the college is that most faculty members will have demanding departmental administrative responsibilities—service on one or more departmental committees, for example, or even service as chairman for several years.

## THE LADDER TO TENURE

The faculty is also organized by rank. College teachers come in several levels of prestige: full professor, associate professor, assistant professor, lecturer, instructor, and teaching assistant or teaching fellow, in descending order. As in most professions, college teachers usually begin their careers at the bottom rung. Climbing from rank to rank is certainly not their only purpose, but it is one of the ways their profession measures accomplishment.

Another way of defining and rewarding accomplishment is to grant a teacher tenure. The topic of tenure is worth pausing on, since you will confront the following scene more than once during your time in college. You hear from other students that both Latissimus and Scrivener are up for tenure in sociology and that only one of them can get it. Latissimus knows his stuff, by all accounts. He is a charismatic lecturer, a part-time fencing coach, and the author of many journal articles in his field. Scrivener, on the other hand, is severe and quite dry in the classroom, isn't involved much with students, and has written only two books, though both of them have been reviewed in the *New York Times*. Scrivener gets tenure, Latissimus does not, and students write letters to the president of the university asking her to reconsider. Their letters have no effect. What is going on here?

Tenure is permanent appointment to the faculty—the prize young faculty members work for. It signifies that the person has been evaluated by his or her peers and found worthy. The faculty have said in effect: Our young colleague's research, scholarship, and teaching come up to our standards. He or she is capable of teaching the very best of our students and will still be current in our academic field 20 years from now. Tenure carries commitment, status, and security, but, most important, it carries the message that the professor's work is highly respected by people in a position to judge it.

If tenure is a goal to work toward, it is also an event to move beyond. Very few college teachers stop working hard after earning tenure, even though their jobs are secure. Their research continues to demand devotion and performance for the rest of their professional lives. A biologist working on an important problem won't be able to stop working on it just because he has been given tenure. The problem is still there to be solved; the laboratory team is still working on it, and there are still papers to be read at meetings of national professional organizations and proposals to be written to foundations asking for money to support further work. Friends and colleagues in the same specialty in biology have high hopes for his research, and he has pride in what he has been able to accomplish so far.

Sometimes faculty members do stop once they have tenure. They meet their classes, recycle yellowing lecture notes, and tend their roses. This is rare.

## The Purpose of Tenure

The practice of tenure was developed by colleges at the turn of the century to protect the academic freedom of individual professors. Steps for promotion to tenure were spelled out by the American Association of University Professors in the 1930s, as a way of removing young faculty members who were not measuring up. It protects the right of faculty members to work on politically unpopular ideas and to take intellectual risks. There was—and is—always the possibility that a scholar working on the frontier of a field will come to believe something that is not popular with more powerful people or will say something in the classroom that seems to some others to undermine an important tradition or political value. The rule of tenure ensures that teachers will not be fired because, in the course of their work, they discover truths that others don't approve of. So in this way too, tenure is precious; it protects academic freedom.

When the faculty grants tenure to a colleague, they are saying not only that the person's work should be protected (as all academic work should), but also that it should proceed at this college. When they deny tenure, they are not saying that the person's work is not good enough to be protected but that it does not serve the academic strengths the college is developing or that it simply is not good enough to be carried on at their college. They have made a judgment about all aspects of the younger professor's work, including teaching, research, and publication, and found it wanting.

A professor's teaching is almost always part of what is evaluated in the tenure process. Depending on the size and purpose of the college, teaching may not be the most important aspect being evaluated, so a good teacher whose research is judged not good enough will not be tenured, while a less competent teacher whose research is important and whose writing is superb may be given a lifetime job. Each case will upset some students who know the teacher's work in the classroom and have strong opinions about it. Students' perspectives on the person's teaching may count for quite a lot in the tenure process (there may not be many others who know anything about the teaching), but other perspectives concerning research and writing may crowd the opinions of students out of the final assessment.

The tenure decision will usually be made toward the end of a person's term as assistant or associate professor. At some colleges it is possible to earn tenure but never be promoted after that to full professor. That might be the way the college expresses its disappointment with the person's waning scholarly energy and accomplishments. If tenure is denied in the first place, the young scholar usually has a year or two to find a job at another college.

## PROFESSORIAL CAREERS

Think again about the kinds of early impressions you will have of your college teachers. What sort of person sets out to become the teacher you meet in lecture and seminar? Who does this sort of work and then submits to judgments of this sort? In this situation more than almost any other presented in this book, it is dangerous to generalize. College professors were once like you. Some of them were smarter than you or thought they were. Some were not and earned grades and scores just like yours. Some hated school. Some didn't go to college until after they had served several years in the army. Some people have become world-class scholars without having graduated from college. Some were exactly like the people in your high school class you think will become professors—shy, introverted, obsessed with star gazing or computer projects of various kinds, or tending terrifying pet reptiles. Some chose between careers as theoretical physicists, specializing in the theory of gravitation, and careers as professional golfers. Some chose more prosaically—a Ph.D. in American Studies over law school. At least one recruited football player discovered the mathematical beauty of certain chemical reactions and went on to win the Nobel prize.

Some professors will say they chose the academic life because they are uncomfortable around other people and would prefer the library or the laboratory to the hurly-burly of clients and customers and buying and selling. This is true of some academic people, certainly, but don't make the mistake of assuming it is true of all. There are no safe generalizations along these lines. You may be as likely as anyone else your age to become a professor someday, especially if some academic project sneaks up on you and takes hold of your imagination.

## A Professor's Training

Almost all of your college teachers have gone to graduate school in the subject they are teaching. The path to the Ph.D. (the formal name of the degree is Doctor of Philosophy) leads through a year or two of additional course work and a short master's thesis, to preliminary research on a dissertation topic, then to a formal dissertation proposal to a faculty committee, and finally to further research and writing the dissertation. Usually a dissertation is a book-length, publishable essay, in which the graduate student has made an original contribution to scholarship in the field. Once the faculty committee has accepted the dissertation, the university confers the doctorate. It can take four years to a decade or more to complete this work. Members of a college faculty may still be working on their doctorates while teaching. Sometimes a member of a faculty will have an advanced degree other than a doctorate—a degree in law or medicine, for example, or a second master's.

## Scholarly Research

Teaching and learning in college are deeply affected by the work professors are doing when they are not in the classroom trying to teach you something. The following list will give you an idea of the sorts of topics faculty members work on that may or may not be topics of courses they are teaching: the history of the ancient Mayas in Copan and Honduras, Vietnam's emerging legal system, Arabic drama and politics in the 1950s, the theory of the equatorial undercurrent, physics with hadron colliders, gender and ethnicity in the Jewish immigrant community of London in the years 1880–1939, competition and cooperation between Japan and the United States, human rights and low-intensity conflict in the Philippines. A professor offering a course three mornings a week in the history of the shogun in Japan is working on the Sumo tradition in the afternoons. Another, who has just published an article on the Sanskrit sources for the study of Varanasi, teaches a course introducing students to Buddhism. A professor whose popular course is on the modern novel has just finished five years of work on a book that is a critical reading of James Joyce, Virginia Woolf, and D.H. Lawrence. A theoretical astrophysicist teaches a physics course in which students do almost no math but write two essays a week. A professor who has written scholarly articles on terrorism, the use of deadly force by police, contemporary politics, prison, and punishment offers a course in crime and society.

Sometimes a professor's scholarly work feeds directly into his or her courses; sometimes the connection is less clear. In the best case, moving back and forth between the classroom and the library keeps the mind active and the vocabulary flexible, keeps the material of a course fresh and current, and in a large course where there is a staff of section teachers, provides a scholarly framework within which to train less-expert teachers. Research can enhance teaching, and students who are intellectually curious can often get to know world-class scholars.

> *Contrary to popular belief, I discovered that most professors are extremely accessible and are willing to discuss their studies with any interested students. In fact, I was one of only nine students in a freshman seminar taught by a prize-winning physicist. Not only do I now understand the work involved in becoming one of the world's great scientists (and the consequences thereof), but my professor even found me a summer job as a counselor in a math-and-science program in France!*

All of this may help clarify the largest professional difference between high school teacher and college professor. Ordinarily, the profession of the high school teacher is teaching, English or physics, for example. The profession of the professor is, in the literary case, critic, historian, linguist, philosopher, and writer; in the scientific case, inventor, engineer, philosopher, and physicist. Each profession has its own standards of excellence, but teaching is only part of what professors do.

It is fair to say that the faculty is the college. You will be in college for four or five years, but tenured faculty members serve for a lifetime and are the continuity and the memory of the place. Faculty members must take on more college responsibilities than just teaching and conducting research. They fill senior administrative posts: they are the provost, the dean of the faculty, the dean of the graduate school, the dean of the college. They serve on standing committees like admissions, examinations and standing, curriculum, promotion and tenure, budget, discipline, and sponsored research, and on ad hoc committees (sometimes with students) on particular issues like freedom of speech, sexual harassment, or race relations.

## Professors as "People"

Remember when you saw your fourth-grade teacher at the grocery store for the first time and suddenly realized that teachers, or at least this one, had lives outside school and didn't live in a classroom cupboard overnight? Or when you saw your French teacher at a football game and were struck by the possibility that he had interests other than irregular verbs? You will catch similar, perhaps even more intimate, glimpses into the lives of your college teachers. Your roommate will be invited to babysit for his history professor's children and will come back to the room announcing that he has a crush on the professor's wife. You will see your psychology instructor, pushing a stroller across the main quadrangle, stop to confer with a colleague who is leaning out of a third-floor window of a faculty office building and suddenly flip that colleague, in all good humor, an internationally familiar crude gesture. A friend will report that the English teacher who has just returned your paper on Emerson for the second time, saying it is unsatisfactory and asking for further revision, is seen every spring afternoon watching baseball practice. Your adviser will invite you to dinner and you will be served mushrooms and green peas—that's all—by her obviously loony husband. The professor in your modern novel course, trying to illustrate a point about characters in certain books who take on roles, will describe a game his children play. Or the leader of your freshman seminar in astronomy will discover that you share an interest in mountain climbing and will show you slides of her most recent expedition to Mount Rainier.

You may have several experiences like this in college but still feel they are not the norm. Usually faculty members will count on you to reach out to them—to talk to them after class or to seek them out during office hours. They have other work to do in addition to teaching you, and they must get to it. In turn, they will assume that you have a life outside their courses (though the load of work they assign may suggest otherwise) and may be shy about intruding into your world. Most faculty members will be quite awkward at large parties given by students and will look for excuses to leave early or not accept invitations in the first place. Even tea in a dormitory common room, or dinner at a fraternity or sorority house before an informal talk about the faculty member's newest research interest or collection of poems can be extremely hard for some faculty. Try to understand this before lending your voice to a general chorus of complaints about lack of contact with the faculty.

## Professorial Distractions

You will find out early how difficult it is to write a paper without interruption. You can't write at the library without being asked by someone else how your paper is coming. You can't write in the room without being asked if you want some popcorn fresh from the popper. Imagine what it is like for the professor while he or she is trying to grade your paper. An editor is on the phone, or a representative of a government agency, or a colleague on the opposite coast wanting help setting up next month's symposium. At home, dinner needs to be cooked, the dog needs to be walked, and a diaper needs to be changed—all at the same time. So a piece of work done by you in the midst of your everyday distractions is evaluated by the faculty member in the midst of his or hers. The exchange between you is carried out in a way neither of you might like. All the more reason to have a conversation with your instructor after your work is returned to you, so you can hear more about what you have done.

## WHAT IS GOOD TEACHING?

How do you know whether you are being well taught? Since college itself is a new world for you and the scholarly work and other commitments of your teachers will be mostly invisible to you, how can you tell? This is a question to ask in college precisely because you are so much more responsible for the quality and direction of your own education than you were in high school. Try out the following notions as answers to the question.

- You are being well taught when complex ideas are made clear without losing their complexity and when simple ideas are discussed without becoming unnecessarily complex.
- You are being well taught when you begin to see connections and relationships between things because of something a teacher has said or because of a situation (an assignment, for example) that a teacher has set up.
- You are being well taught when you feel invited to improvise and to think clearly and responsibly at the same time.

Still, you probably won't really know whether you've been well taught by particular college teachers until long after you've left college. Five or ten years later, you may see what was going on in a course and realize you didn't appreciate it at the time. For now, you may decide that it's best to come to judgments that are only tentative—about this professor's apparent command of the material, that one's style of lecturing, and how that other conducts a class discussion. A teacher who is eccentric, or distracted by career ambitions, or involved in her own work, or even not very entertaining may still teach you extraordinarily well.

Often, the ways teachers and students work on the subject matter, the stuff, of a course can be quite satisfactory.

*Although I took mainly large lecture courses this semester, I was very impressed with the amount of individual attention that I received from teaching fellows and even from professors. Everyone seemed to make an extra effort to be accessible to students, usually giving us their home phone numbers and encouraging us to get in touch with them if we had any questions at all. My freshman writing teacher spent nearly 45 minutes a week with me in her office, going over my writing. My math teacher gave his own review sessions every week in addition to his three weekly lectures and office hours and the course assistant's review sessions. Whenever I had questions, I felt comfortable going to see him in his office, since he always made time to help me, even on short notice. When I needed help with a whole new concept, he spent however long it took with me until I understood it, even if that was an hour.*

*In our moral reasoning course, the pitch of argument and learning and curiosity became so high as we studied for our exam that we called our professor (we—two of my roommates and I—members of a class of 400 people!) to talk about some of his theories . . . and a few days after the exam, took him out for coffee and a two-hour philosophical discussion that was thrilling and soul searching and educational in the best possible sense of the word.*

*Two roads diverged in a wood, and I—*
*I took the one less traveled by,*
*And that has made all the difference.*
(Robert Frost)

# 10
## Choosing a Major

You will probably be asked to declare a major toward the end of your second year. In some colleges the moment will come earlier. The choice is one of a constellation of decisions you will make in college—courses each term, roommates after the first year, topics for course papers and independent work, whether to continue with particular extracurricular activities, which dormitory to live in or whether to live off campus. But the choice of a major is as important, and in some of the same ways, as the decision about which college to attend and may carry almost as many mistaken assumptions—in this case, about why a particular major is right for you. It's useful, therefore, to think about the question early, not in order to settle it but to identify the main considerations and then at least make a tentative choice.

The faculty issues this challenge of choosing a major to you with several purposes in mind. They want you to have some practice at making important choices on your own. They want you to have at least a taste of what it's like to do scholarly work using the basic tools of an academic discipline. They believe that undergraduate work should have not only good breadth but real depth in some one thing. They want you to focus your reading and research and sharpen your writing and calculating, so that you can begin to feel what mastery of a subject might be like. They do not think of majoring in a field as preparing you for a particular trade, nor, in most cases, will it be helpful for you to think about it this way.

Any choice you make may be questioned by someone.

> *The course offerings are fabulous—I've discovered that I love history (contrary to previous beliefs) and have decided to major in the history and literature of modern France and England. When I tell my relatives about my choice, they wonder what I can do with such a seemingly restrictive major. Most wonder what kind of job I can expect to find besides teaching. But that's the whole magic of college— you can do anything your heart desires with your four years here. I've decided to study what fascinates me, not what I feel I should study to prepare for my future career. I know that in order to go to business school I don't need to*

*concentrate in economics and that to go to law school I don't need government courses. College has helped me see the future in a different light. I know now that my choices are unlimited. I want to work abroad—in France or England—for an international company or law firm. That's my dream—to travel, work with interesting people, and be my own boss some day. And I know I can do it! I just have to follow my instincts and do what feels right to me, not what others say I should do.*

## EARLY EXPLORATION

We can justify including a discussion of choosing a major in a book that is otherwise about the transition from school to college, because a satisfying choice will depend on explorations that ought to start as soon as possible. For the time being, you should take the idea of exploration seriously. A minimum of a quarter of your courses will be in your major field, so it makes sense to work at finding something that you will enjoy, first of all, and that will also let you achieve some of your goals for your education. It may be tempting to tag yourself a bio or a lit major or someone working in appl math, psych, or anthro, because the tag will make you seem purposeful and knowledgeable. "Undecided" sounds pretty undecided, after all (even if you joke that you are undecided but serious about it). The tag will be useful if it provides you with a point of departure and maybe even a point of return, but it should not be used as a reason to ignore alternatives. And it should certainly not represent an unthinking, uncritical commitment to a field that you really don't know the shape of, nor should it be the case that the choice isn't yours so much as your parents' or that of someone else who wants the "very best" for you. So even if you think you know what you want to do, approach it with an open mind, since one of the most exciting things about college is the way you can be taken by surprise. If you are undecided, flaunt it—college will suddenly become an open-air market, everybody offering you something of value. This is not to suggest that being undecided is not painful. It hurts to recognize that you're going to have to make a decision, eliminate some things you'd like to try, or choose between equally uninteresting alternatives.

## Means of Exploring

How do you set out to explore possible majors? Often there will be such literature as a course catalog, a special handbook, or departmental brochures in which the fields are described. The handbook will list the faculty and their areas of expertise, the number and kinds of courses required for a degree in a given department, cognate (related) courses, the opportunities for independent work and for honors, and perhaps even what recent graduates have gone on to do. It will also describe the possibilities for double majors or joint majors with other departments.

Not surprisingly, the most useful tools for making the decision of a major are the courses you take that reveal that you could be happy or unhappy in a particular field, and other students' stories of what it feels like to be concentrating in a given field. This means that every course you take in the first year or two has the potential to say something to you about majoring. The course may demand that you read and write in a way you enjoy, that you think precisely, or that you make oral presentations, which appeals to you—excellent reasons for considering a major. Other students you meet in class, at glee club practice, or on the playing field will give you glimpses into their departments. Listen to them. You may decide to explore a direction you never thought of until you had such an accidental conversation. There are many more fields in college than those that are familiar to you from high school, and it may take time and effort to persuade yourself that you can enjoy working in a field you don't know much about. You may also find yourself settling the question in a way that takes you by surprise.

> *As of this spring, my concentration is visual and environmental studies, even though I came here to do engineering. My choice to concentrate in this field is*

> *supported mainly by the fact that the visual arts give me something that is always enjoyable and the idea of a visual arts–related career is one that I have entertained for years. Considering that I had never heard of visual and environmental studies when I got here, I wonder whether my choice is right. However, I plan to also try to meet the premed requirements.*

Deans and faculty members may collaborate on interest meetings for potential majors. Representatives from the departments will review what is in the catalogs, faculty members will describe their courses and research, students will discuss their work, and people thinking about majoring in the different areas will be able to ask questions. Go to as many of those meetings as make sense for you. And take advantage of faculty members' office hours to get their recommendations about courses that may be especially appropriate introductions to a field.

Don't assume there are conventional, preferred links between certain fields and certain careers. If you want to go into medicine, you need not major in biology or chemistry. Law schools do not insist that people major in political science, and business schools admit many people who did not choose economics. If you study English or philosophy, you are not fated to teach. We should look at why all this is so. But first let's approach the question from another angle and look at some stories about people who discovered that an apparent lack of connection among original plans for college, eventual choice of major, and ultimate career path or paths did not doom them to lives of aimless wandering.

## **MAKING THE CHOICE**

Earlier, in Chapter 2, we touched briefly on the story of a young man named Anton. Anton decided late in high school, partly because he had been told that he was a talented draftsman and partly because of family tradition, that he wanted to become an architect. Until then, though he had thought about commercial art and the law, the only career he was vehemently opposed to considering was education. He announced to all who would listen that he would never teach. But he was uncertain enough about architecture that he wanted to go to a college where he could change his mind about his major without having to apply all over again for admission to another division of the college, as might have been the case at some universities with professional training programs in architecture at the undergraduate level.

He was admitted to a suitable college and, in short order, discovered that the architecture program there was not what he wanted after all, so he left the program. He flirted briefly with the idea of political science and finally chose English. He loved to read and to think and talk about great books. He also knew he had some aptitude. He minored in a special program in American Studies.

Early in his senior year, not knowing what to do next, he took the Law School Aptitude Test, applied to three law schools, and was accepted by two of them. The admissions representative of the third school had the honesty to say to Anton that he didn't really seem to want to go to law school; Anton was honest enough to admit that it was so. But he sent his room deposit to the school he preferred and began to prepare himself mentally to become a lawyer.

It happened that Anton had come under the influence of one of his English professors from whom he had taken three or four courses and who was the adviser of his senior independent work. During the course of that year, it slowly dawned on Anton that he was fascinated by the mysteries of teaching. How was it that someone could teach anything to anyone else? In March of his senior year, he decided to apply to a graduate program in American literature to find out whether he also had that ability. He was admitted and immediately wrote to the law school asking for his room deposit. The bursar refused to refund it. Anton went off to graduate school, grumbling about being $300 short before he started. This was the young man who in high school had sworn to anyone who would listen that he was never, ever going to teach.

## Following Different Paths

Several more stories follow that tell of apparent non sequiturs. Can you imagine connections that aren't visible on the surface?

Rae came to college after spending two summers working in a restaurant in her native Chicago. She loved the work and the situations she encountered in the restaurant business, so she decided to major in economics in college and go into the business, hoping someday to run her own restaurant. She clung to this goal until the end of the fall semester of her junior year when, as she was about to go beyond the intermediate level in economics, she decided that she hated the field.

Without admitting it to herself before this, Rae had begun to fall in love with comparative literature. Now, quickly but carefully, she began to consult with instructors in courses that had been important to her and with deans and other advisers whom she had come to trust during her first two years. Following those consultations, she switched fields, giving up economics and transferring to literature. Her remaining semesters were intellectually exciting and satisfying. Rae wrote an honors thesis on two African-American writers.

Rae's experience would be interesting enough if we left the story there. But in the spring of her senior year, while she was finishing her thesis, she was interviewed by several investment banking firms. She applied for three postgraduate traveling fellowships, but she didn't win any, so she decided to work for one of the investment firms. She spent the next two years learning the intricacies of leveraged buyouts. In the fall of the second year, she decided to wanted to do graduate work in literature, earn a doctorate, and teach. The plan for the restaurant would just have to wait, she concluded, until she decided she didn't like teaching and scholarship after all.

Michael was determined at the outset to major in architecture as an undergraduate and then go on to graduate school in design. He failed the freshman physics course that was required of architecture majors and so was at loose ends for several semesters. He had been a solid distance runner in high school but on a whim had gone out for crew after he had been at college for a few weeks. While he was uncertain of what to do academically, he became a member of a boat crew that was eventually two-time national champion and raced twice at Henley, England. Meanwhile, he took a religion course from a professor who was the father of one of his friends from summer camp. Persuaded by that teacher and his course, he decided to major in religion. He had knit up his loose ends.

He graduated from college something of an expert on fundamentalist Islam. He coached his college's crew team part-time for a year, took a physics course, and worked as an apprentice in an architect's office, getting ready to go to graduate school in design.

Midway through her freshman year, Jo went to her adviser in something of a panic. She had mapped out her four years of courses and discovered that if she was going to complete the requirements for admission to medical school and major in biology, she was going to have to give up music. Jo had been a talented singer and voice student during high school. Her adviser suggested that she set out to follow her plan but right now, in the second semester of her first year, also take the most wonderful music course she could find. Jo enrolled in a conducting course. Eight years later she was the artistic director of a major opera company.

Leo came to college recruited to play football. He had considerable academic ability but no very strong intellectual interest. When the time came to talk with his adviser about choosing a major, Leo announced he was going to concentrate in East Asian studies. The adviser was baffled. Leo had shown no interest in the field and had no background in it. When the adviser asked why, Leo explained that they had said a small department was better and that this was a small department. He didn't explain who "they" were nor would he be dissuaded. Two years later, he was flourishing in East Asian studies, taking second-year Japanese—and playing excellent football.

Margaret told her freshman adviser that she was going to major in Spanish and do as much work as she could in international affairs both in and out of the classroom, because she wanted eventually to work for the State Department as a specialist in Latin America. She followed that plan meticulously until the middle of her senior year, when she was recruited by a New York brokerage firm. Immediately after graduation, she went to New York and worked for three years, helping to arrange large and important deals. After three years, having hated almost every minute of the brokerage life, she quit, got married, and returned to her native New Hampshire to teach school, happily ever after—for the time being.

George decided early in college to major in philosophy. He loved the rigor of the subject. It was wonderfully exciting to him to labor through the work of the great thinkers and develop ideas critically and skeptically in response to theirs. For some time, George had in the back of his mind the idea of becoming a doctor. During the summer between his first and second years, he took a volunteer job in a hospital, where he had the opportunity to watch doctors at their ordinary work and, as an orderly, to involve himself in a minor way in the life of the hospital. In the fall, he came back to school enthusiastic about medicine and made a plan for meeting his premed requirements while completing a philosophy major. In the summer between his sophomore and junior years, he took a job in a laboratory, helping with basic research in immunology. When he returned to school that fall, he switched majors to biochemistry and, during the course of his senior year, applied both to medical schools and to M.D.–Ph.D. programs so he could continue to do research. The intellectual challenge that had been so important to him as a philosophy major motivated his continuing commitment to science.

There are many routine stories of the English major who goes to work for a publishing house, the biology major who becomes a doctor, the political science major who goes to law school, or the accounting major who becomes a CEO. The students in these less-usual stories didn't necessarily have happier and more fulfilling college experiences. What is important to note is that the unusual paths they took were not linear. In fact, they seem braided or even, like the double helix, really not paths at all but routes with several dimensions. The point made in all the stories that trace these peculiar routes is that choosing a major does not necessarily commit a person to particular next steps or even to a particular range of options. Your purposes will change and your intentions will rise and fall in continuing counterpoint; you will experience accidents, discoveries, inventions, and changing relationships and still feel as though you are moving through a coherent career. In other words, there are many ways of getting to the future that do not lie along a straight line.

## Pitfalls and Possibilities

What is sometimes hard about choosing your major is the distinct feeling that the possibilities for your life are diminishing, that there are things you will never do because you have made this choice. It's probably true; by opting for anthropology you may be giving up the chance to do serious mathematics, though even this is not necessarily so. On the other hand, you will be discovering fields, ways of thinking about the world, and possibilities for adventure, intellectual and otherwise, that you might not have known otherwise. Such choices almost always produce new chances at the same time old possibilities are eliminated. Whatever decisions you make, stay alert to what you like, to what satisfies you intellectually and in other ways, so that giving something up can be simply a consequence of a positive choice.

People often look toward choosing a major in one of two ways—either dead set on their major before they get to college and unwavering after they arrive or mired in indecision. Overcommitment settles the question—but maybe too early. Refusing to choose protects you from the consequences of choosing. So the challenge to your imagination is to find a middle ground—exploring with an open mind, understanding that the choice of a major won't determine the rest of your life, being willing finally to hold your nose and jump, admitting that some things about your chosen field will be bad and some things good. Then you can answer the question "What if I don't like my major?" by assuring yourself that you can change, and the question

"Haven't I closed a lot of doors?" by seeing that you have also opened many. Finally, there is nothing to do but choose and take the aftermath step by step, even though narrowing your field and committing yourself may be difficult.

> *September 22. Excerpt from a letter to my mother: I keep turning the doctor profession over and over in my head. This is a really confusing time for me. There are a good number of people who are here just to enjoy—and to learn things they have always wanted to learn. They don't seem to feel pressured about grades and competition. How ideal. Right now I feel caught between two extremes. I definitely want to prepare for a career, but I have reservations about medicine. I really don't feel that I have the capacity to be a practically straight-A student. I really think I'd like to major in biochem. If med school fails me—which I'm convinced it will—then I could always get a Ph.D. It's so complex. What should I do? Do you and Dad have any advice? I know it's still early, but it's good to know where you're going.*

> *September 24. Excerpt from a letter to my father: Thanks for your letter. You're right. I'm here to enjoy these four years, not to agonize over them. Apparently, to many people college is the climax to their lives. I'm sure it will be hard for me. If I do my best and work hard (but not too hard), I'm confident I'll do well. I'm surprised that, although there are many kids here who are intellectually superior to me, there are also many kids below my level. I feel pretty secure.*

## AFTER YOU'VE MADE THE CHOICE

Let's look again at the experience of concentrating in a particular department. Try to imagine what it will be like to work with a small group of faculty members, one of whom will be your adviser, in a structured program demanding that you cover a defined body of material. You will have opportunities to do independent work, which will be different in several ways from course work. You will have the opportunity to take comprehensive exams to show that you have mastered the material of the major. You will have a chance to graduate with honors. What are the challenges of the actual experience?

As we've said, courses in your major will probably make up at least 25 percent of all your course work, a significant fraction of what you must do to earn the degree. It is relatively easy to choose a set of courses that will satisfy the requirements of your department, much less easy to make a plan that gives you a balanced view of the field, and even harder to choose courses outside your major that will complement what you do in the department and still allow you breadth of study. The department will assign you to an adviser, or may even let you choose somebody, and you should take advantage of that person's expertise by consulting regularly about your choice of courses and the material of the courses you choose. If it is possible to do independent work as an upperclassman, your adviser may be the person who reads your papers or evaluates other sorts of assignments—lab work, for example. You will learn more from those evaluations if they are part of a working relationship than if they occur at rare meetings of almost perfect strangers.

## Independent Research

Independent work will be one of your greatest challenges; you may be left more alone than you want, from the moment of inventing a topic through establishing a reading list to completing the project. After handing in a 25-page paper on military behavior in the carpenter ant, you may not be ready to hear that the definitive scholarly book on your topic was published just six months ago. So you might ask your adviser to help you pick a topic on which you can do satisfying work and to help steer your research, especially the first time or two out, so that you don't run aground. After that, you really may want to be on your own. If you find that working independently is demanded by your major, you will want to choose courses in your freshman and sophomore years that prepare you to do the sort of independent study required. If you arrive at the department never having written up a substantial piece of research and so are completely unprepared to build on the work of others, the going may be rougher than necessary for a while.

If you are a candidate for honors, you may have a chance to write a thesis in your senior year. Senior theses take different forms, but an undergraduate thesis in the humanities and social sciences may be anywhere from 50 to 250 pages, including footnotes and bibliography that take up roughly 5 to 15 pages. A thesis in the natural sciences may involve working on a discrete portion of a large experiment for several months, risking failure of the experiment, and doing a thorough survey of the literature and a write-up of the laboratory work. For many people, the thesis is the proof of their undergraduate education, testing and integrating everything they have learned.

Senior theses may be on a variety of topics. You may write on religious authority and political modernization in Saudi Arabia, analogues of Arthurian romance in *Moby Dick*, feminist politics and the writings of Arendt and Habermas. You may design, construct, and calibrate a photoacoustic calorimeter, theorize about Thomas Gainsborough's varnished watercolor technique, or write a novel called *The Two-Edged Sword*.

Your relationship with your thesis adviser can be the most important of your college years—and not just as a way of developing a mentor and sponsor for whatever may come next. Your adviser can be the college teacher from whom you learn the most, because you are collaborating on a project rather than giving or taking a course.

You will have other opportunities for integrating what you have learned in a balanced and thorough exploration of your field. General or comprehensive examinations (also known as generals) are often given, in addition to regular course exams, at the end of the upperclass years. These generals may be tests of guided work or reading you have done, or perhaps they will be tests of what you know, with no reading list to work from. Whatever the case, you will probably find course material that seemed more or less disconnected before you began to study for these exams now begins to fit together, and you can even see how to fill the gaps.

## Honors

Sometimes, the option to sit for general exams or to write a thesis will be offered only to candidates for honors. What does an honors program involve? Usually there will be additional requirements for the degree: 10 courses instead of 8, for example. Often a particular level of achievement will be set, such as no grade lower than a B in a departmental course. Sometimes you will have to declare yourself a candidate for honors when you join the department and so move along a different track from the one traveled by candidates for the degree without honors. Sometimes honors will simply be calculated by the faculty of the department once you have completed all the requirements for the major. Traditionally there are three levels of honors: cum laude, magna cum laude, and summa cum laude. If you earn honors, one of these phrases will be attached to your degree: B.A. in mathematics, magna cum laude. Again, the reason to consider this early on is that the decision to compete for honors may have to be made at the same time you choose your major and could, in fact, affect your choice, depending on the requirements for honors in the fields you are considering.

## UNCONVENTIONAL MAJORS

What happens to people whose academic interests are so broad or specialized or complex that they cannot be satisfied by study in a single department? In most colleges, you can declare a minor or create the equivalent of a minor by choosing courses in a certain configuration. There are also opportunities for double majors (a degree for which you complete the major requirements in two departments), joint majors (a degree for which you complete the requirements set by a special committee with members from more than one department), and special majors (a degree in a field whose boundaries and requirements you set with the approval of a faculty committee). For most students, the demands of an established department or program are rigorous enough and provide sufficient opportunity for work of breadth and depth, but the flexibility usually exists for the student with special interests to combine or even invent unique courses of study.

## A WARNING

We can't end this chapter without reissuing the strongest caveat of all: Beware of assumptions about the payoff from your college major. Career paths might be better explored in summer jobs or internships than in an academic department. No matter how often you hear that a particular major is favored by a particular sort of graduate or professional school or by particular sorts of employers, be skeptical until you hear it from the horse's mouth. Medical schools will say they care less about a particular major than they do about the capacity for dealing with other people and for solving particular kinds of problems. Law schools will tell you it doesn't matter whether it was political science, philosophy, or English, so long as you learned to read critically, write clearly, and argue persuasively and with conviction. Business schools will want to see evidence of your ability to think analytically and signs of a high level of energy. Employers will often say that the choice of major doesn't matter at all, so long as you can think, talk, and write well and learn to crunch numbers.

These are not rules either, but impressions shared by experienced observers of various postbaccalaureate worlds. Test them out, as you would any assertion, rather than letting assumptions about what is required govern your choices in college and lead you to study things for which you have no passion whatsoever. The sort of person almost everybody will be looking for after graduation is one who has taken the opportunities provided by a college education to sharpen all of his or her intellectual and personal skills and to develop a clear vision of how he or she wants to live. The one career path for which your major will be important will be the one that leads to further work in that field at the master's or doctoral level. Even so, many people have gone on to do advanced work in a field different from the one they majored in. If you think about it, that's very natural, since people's intellectual interests are no more static than any other part of their lives. Students of biochemistry do go on to become psychotherapists or retailers.

Keep in mind, as you consider the prospect of choosing a major, that the choice is not so different from other choices you will make many times in college; it makes the most sense when it is done in the context of finding or confirming your sense of educational purpose. If you make the effort, choosing will be meaningful, and work in your field in college is likely to be at least satisfying and at best inspiring.

*She was the single artificer of the world
In which she sang.*
                              (Wallace Stevens)

*I think of games as social fictions, like works of art, which exist only as long as they are continuously created. They are like plays or songs or dances, belonging to some special sphere of human activity which clearly lies outside the normal reality of day-to-day living.*
                              (Bernard De Koven)

*Tradition is a matter of much wider significance. It cannot be inherited, and if you want it you must obtain it by great labour.*
                              (T. S. Eliot)

# 11
# *Making Extracurricular Commitments*

For fun—for the sheer joy of the thing. Because others expect it of you. To meet friends. Because you've always been involved and active. For a change of pace from academic work. Because you thrive on competition. To round out your college experience. To develop skills you know you have. To see whether you are any good at something you haven't done before. To improve your chances for admission to law school. To try out a role you might want to take on someday in the "real world." To pursue excellence.

These are some of the reasons you might give for wanting to participate in extracurricular activities in college. Indeed, these are most of the reasons extracurricular activities exist in college, since societies of various kinds, and even athletic teams, were founded by students.

The range of activities probably will be wider in college than in high school, so there will be more choice. The opportunities will run deeper, too, in the sense that you will be able to do more, learn more, and take on greater leadership responsibility. But the days are gone when you can fool around kicking a football while warming up for cross-country practice, hear from the football coach that you can kick farther than anybody he's got on his team at the moment, and suit up for Saturday's game. Gone too is the possibility of being named art editor of the newspaper in exchange for drawing just one topical cartoon each month. The competition will be stiffer in college (there may be 10 other cartoonists, and both the punter and his backup probably will be former all-conference players), and the competition will produce specialists and experts. So although you will be able to choose both from activities that are familiar and those that are new to you, you will probably find that you have to focus more sharply because the demands on your time and energy will be so much greater.

## CHOOSING AND BALANCING

Students react to the challenge in different ways.

*The college gave me more activities to try than I could ever hope to sample, but I ended up pursuing music almost*

> *exclusively. I have no regrets, only a sense of loss for the plays and magazines I never got to try out for. How can anyone balance it all?*
>
> *It seems that I kept up my high school habit of putting schoolwork before everything else this semester. But I've often asked myself whether this is right. Is this what college is supposed to be like? Everyone says no, you go to college for the "experience." At the same time, though, I know that the education will be most important to me in later life. What I actually seek is a balance of studying and other activities that will be both enjoyable and educational.*

The purpose of this chapter is to describe the variety of extracurricular opportunities in college and to explore the relationships and tensions between such activities and your academic work. To call something "extracurricular," after all, defines the curricular as central and first priority, but this is not to say that the extracurricular is extraneous or irrelevant. Not to take extracurricular opportunities—at least some of them—seriously, as an integral part of your education, would be a mistake. On the other hand, college activities can be awfully seductive.

> *I am not sure that I actually spend more time on school work here. As a matter of fact, I probably spend less time than I used to. What surprised me was how difficult a working environment I found the college to be, because of the incredibly wide range of distractions it offers. I am not complaining about this fact; the many opportunities are probably my favorite part about life here. It is simply difficult to find enough time to study when surrounded by so many other ways to spend one's time.*

A taxonomy, or classification, may help us see more clearly how many distractions there are.

## Arts

With a little exploration and nagging, you may find that there is studio space for both painting and sculpture—and maybe even a person or two (other students perhaps) willing to provide instruction. You may find places for craftsmanship as well—a pottery studio or an old hand-operated printing press sitting forgotten in the basement of a college building. In music, you will immediately see invitations everywhere (including the calendar of orientation week events) to audition for the glee club, the madrigal society, the bands (marching, concert, and jazz), the orchestra and several chamber groups, and the small close-harmony singing groups that seem to embody the traditions of the college. Opportunities in theater will range from drama to musical comedy to opera, together with the technical and public relations work that supports production. There will be modern and jazz dance groups and perhaps even a group that teaches dance to children in the local schools.

## Journalism

You may find opportunities to be a "stringer" for a national or local publication; to compete for a place on the established student newspaper; to work in a more relaxed fashion for the upstart, rival student paper; and to help put out the annual literary magazine, the yearbook, the freshman "face book," and any of several journals connected with academic interest and activity (international affairs, for example).

## Sports

There will be intercollegiate sports, of course, running the gamut from field hockey to basketball, swimming to football, squash to softball. You'll probably also find an intramural program (however informal, it probably will be better organized and more popular than intramurals in high school) that pits dorm against dorm, one fraternity or sorority against another, club against club, and perhaps even faculty against students (the faculty basketball team may even take the championship). Keep an eye out for club sports that haven't been given varsity status by the athletic department (rugby, women's ice hockey, riflery, water polo, volleyball).

## Political Organizations

The chances to express your ideas about politics and even to get some practical experience will be many and varied: Young Republicans and Democrats; groups supporting divestment of shares in companies doing business in South Africa; model congress and model UN programs; student government; environmental groups; joint student-faculty committees on discipline, residential life, and advising are examples of the range that may be offered.

## Service Opportunities

Chances for community service range from work as an RA or a guide for prospective students and their families to joining an organization that sends tutors into local schools or volunteers to nearby hospitals and prisons, takes elderly people on outings to the state park, or provides staff for a soup kitchen or a shelter for the homeless.

## Businesses

A college will often allow certain kinds of entrepreneurial activity—selling mugs and banners, going door to door selling pizza or submarine sandwiches (you might know them as grinders, hoagies, or wedges), or staging rock concerts.

## Special-Interest Groups

Racial and ethnic groups may have political, educational, and arts organizations that invite speakers, publish journals and newsletters, and put on theater and dance performances. There will be religious fellowships sponsored by the campus ministries, women's groups, peer counseling and education groups, and preprofessional societies (law, medicine, and business). Gay and lesbian groups may have established organizations. The debate and chess teams will compete against teams from other colleges.

### Social Organizations

There probably will be fraternities and sororities as well as social clubs of various kinds. And there may be organizations whose purposes are vague and whose qualifications for membership mysterious, such as the Rocky Mountain Club, the Society for Creative Anachronism, the Chinn and Beake, the Gnome, or the X.

## CHOOSING AGAIN

No college's offerings will be exactly like this, but the range is representative. One of the earliest pressures on you will be to decide where to start. It is important to do something early, rather than wait until the rest of college life feels comfortable, for at least three reasons. First, college life may take a while to get comfortable. Second, early practice at balancing the curricular and the extracurricular will stand you in good stead later. And last, this is the realm in which you are most likely to find friends and in which you will come to know and value others because of what they can accomplish in an area of interest that you share. Choosing may be hard, especially if you have been used to participating in many activities in high school. So think about the kinds of balancing acts that you might need to perform—between the familiar and the new, the activity that comes easily and the one that stretches your abilities, the organization that is related to something you might want to do after college and the one that isn't related to any serious purpose, the activity that demands a huge amount of time and the one that doesn't. And though the list seems endless, you may find that you want to do something for which there is no organization at the college, that there is a void in the extracurricular landscape. Don't hesitate to try to start an organization and to approach other students and the college itself for support; you might make quite a splash.

> *When I came to college, I felt like a small fish in a big pond, knowing only where to get food and where to study.*

*As time went on, I really developed a sense for how much of a difference I could make, and, you know, I really feel great about the things I had a chance to do. My roommate and I started an a cappella singing group. When we made the front page of the paper, I was amazed that we had actually pulled it off. Within the next month or so, we had a concert and, only a few months later, came in second at the Intercollegiate Talent Show.*

## A Representative Instance

Let's leave the classification of activities and organizations and consider one activity in some detail. It is typical in many ways of the opportunities college life offers, opportunities that you may not have thought of before. The example is rowing.

Eugene attends a huge public high school in a large city in the Midwest. He is a strong student, especially in math and science. Although he has the tall, wiry body of an athlete, he doesn't participate in sports but spends all his spare time in debate and math competitions. He has no use for athletes and thinks of himself as awkward and without athletic ability. On the weekends, he often takes long, hard bicycle rides, usually by himself, on a bike that he cares for as though it were an heirloom watch and whose every bearing he knows intimately.

After graduating from high school, Eugene goes to a medium-sized university in New England, intending to major in math. He has no particular career plan, no illusions about establishing himself socially; he is happy to be at a place where he will be left alone to pursue his interests. His peace is broken at registration on the Monday of orientation week when a person who identifies himself as the freshman heavyweight crew coach approaches him and urges him to come out for the team. Eugene is not even sure he knows what crew is, except that it involves long boats, being outdoors in all weather, and hard work; his curiosity is piqued, though, and he decides to see what it's all about.

The next afternoon at 2 P.M., he reports to the boathouse. From that moment, his life is changed. Virtually every weekday afternoon, he spends three or four hours rowing or getting ready to row. In the early weeks, practice sessions involve mostly conditioning, flat running or doing circuits up and down the seats of the stadium. He and the other members of the group—which dwindles in size with time and the increasing difficulty of the workouts—are introduced to boats and oars, to hardware and the commands of the coxswain (who directs the crew), but they spend very little time on the water. There are some experienced people in the group who have rowed in prep school, even two or three who are rumored to have had some international competition, and they get a little time on the river with the varsity. But in the fall, everybody is treated the same way, divided into eight-man combinations without regard for ability.

Winter workouts are harder and even less exciting—exercise with free weights and a torture machine called an ergometer. And there are long sessions in the indoor "tanks," which move water past the rowers while they sit on sliding seats, rowing with perforated blades.

Eugene and his teammates go out on the river as soon as the ice breaks up in the spring. There are fewer novice oarsmen now, and even some of the experienced people have dropped out. Membership in the first, second, and third freshman boats begins to sort itself out through a process called seat racing. The members of the squad are getting to know one another very well. They talk with one another about little else but rowing. Friends who are not involved in the sport accuse them, usually with good humor, of speaking in code all the time, about blades, pieces, ergs, moves, the reach, and the catch.

Eugene is shifted by the coach back and forth between the second boat and the first until about halfway through the season, when he settles into the first boat. They race eight times that spring, each race lasting only six and a quarter minutes. Rowing turns out to be 98 percent practice. The hours pay off, though; their boat loses only one early race. Toward the end of the spring, when a trip to the Henley Royal Regatta in England is offered to the One F, as the first freshmen are called, by the Friends of Rowing, they race so hard that often some oarsmen are throwing up or almost unconscious at the finish. Eugene's parents fly in for several races, and a number of classmates become loyal fans and attend every race.

For Eugene, rowing feels like a perfect fit. It calls on his particular kind of strength and stamina. It is precise and challenges him to merge himself with seven other people by mastering a technique and understanding and adhering to tactical plans. He has a group of close friends. The rigid, demanding routines and schedule leave him just enough time for his academic work and campus job. He does B+ work in his courses, except in math where he earns A's, and continues to plan to major in math. The boat wins the trip to Henley, so Eugene gets to see Europe for the first time. He returns home just in time to start his summer job with a computer software firm. On weekends he takes his long, solo bike trips, trying to stay in shape for rowing in the fall.

## What Can Be Learned

Strangely, part of the way Eugene's extracurricular experience represents real possibilities for any freshman lies exactly in its Cinderella progress. Out of curiosity, Eugene tries an activity that he virtually has never heard of before, one that for him exists only in college. He takes up a sport although he has no experience as an athlete and, in fact, has been told (and sees every reason to believe) that he has no athletic ability.

Several close friendships emerge naturally from the group at the boathouse. He begins to master a new discipline. He is forced by the demands of the sport on his time and energy to study efficiently. His financial aid package requires that he have an on-campus job, but because rowing demands so much time, he has to find one that will allow him to study while he works. He runs the risk—and sometimes even recognizes it—of becoming obsessed and of limiting his friendships to other oarsmen because only they understand what his afternoons are like. But for the time being, the pleasures of being part of a close-knit group, being in shape and overcoming pain, following the directions of a coach, having some success at an enterprise in which he shares a large part of the responsibility, and being known and respected for his success outweigh the risks of obsession and exclusiveness for Eugene. He continues to maintain his familiar good grip on mathematics; math keeps him from losing himself completely in the exotic business on the river.

> *Pursuit of the ideal binds rowers together and sets them apart from others. Experiencing the same thing with eight other people bonds them somehow—you get close friends from crew. Close friends and the attraction of chasing the elusive spirit of perfection. As a coxswain, this is what attracts me to crew. It's impossible to do everything right, but the attempt is the attraction, the feeling that maybe tomorrow you will attain perfection. This is what attracted and continues to attract me to the sport—the challenge of sacrifice and the pursuit of perfection. In school, there was always a level that was "good enough"—to make a grade or to earn some honor. In crew, especially for a coxswain, nothing, short of perfection, is good enough. The challenge of seeking perfection, with honors and awards as the by-the-way occurrence rather than an ultimate end, was never so forcefully driven home as in crew.*

## Challenges

Not all extracurricular activities (even sports) are as demanding as rowing, but how demanding they are depends almost entirely on you—how much you love what you are doing, how enthusiastic you are, and how serious. Students are regularly required to withdraw from college for a year because of unsatisfactory academic records caused by overcommitment to something other than study. The range of possible overcommitments matches the range of activities at the college almost exactly: to a musical instrument; to the newspaper; to theater, dance, a sport, politics, or parties. Guarding against letting things fall too far off balance seems essential.

On the other hand, practicing serious commitment also seems essential. Students are in charge of extracurricular activities in college to a much greater extent than is true in high school. In college, the fate of the organization—whether its funding is sufficient and its books well kept, whether its projects succeed, whether it is respected and its traditions continue—depends on its members. In general, if students don't do it, no one will. In a slightly modified way, this is true of sports and the large musical and theatrical groups as well; although the college employs coaches and professional directors and conductors, the captains and managers in athletics, the concert managers in music, and the student producers in theater will be the people who must cope with the day-to-day, inner life of the group. The feeling of being responsible for the health of the organization will be shared widely among the members, although there will be some people, as there were in high school, who really don't care.

In the face of this responsibility, there will be real conflict between curricular and extracurricular obligations from time to time. You will be distracted by serious outside commitments, and you eventually will learn how to drag your attention back to the book lying on the table in front of you in the reading room on the second floor of the library. What won't be so easy, especially in your first year, will be establishing a balance before you've figured out the relative importance of things, when, for example, you have to travel to an athletic contest on the same day you have a required quiz in Spanish.

The instructor in Spanish 101 is under no obligation to excuse you from the quiz just because the director of athletics has scheduled a soccer game 150 miles away at the same time. So walking up to the instructor in class a couple of days earlier and announcing that you have to miss the quiz isn't a good idea. It would probably be much better to talk with your coach first, perhaps even after discussing with the captain how to frame the question. The coach may have come up against this situation before and may know what flexibility is reasonable to hope for from this instructor. It may be that the instructor will insist on your taking the quiz and you'll have to miss the game. Be prepared for this, even though, more often than not, it will be possible to find some arrangement to make up the quiz that is fair to other people in the class.

The same sort of conversation may be required, of course, when you have a 10-page research paper due in freshman writing on the Monday following the weekend you play Yum-Yum in the operetta *The Mikado*. The usual tactic is to ask for an extension on Friday. Don't do it this way. Leave your instructor some room to maneuver. When you first learn the schedule of the Gilbert and Sullivan Players, check your assignment schedule and talk right away with your instructor. It may turn out that the adjustment that makes most sense to you both is for you to write the paper early (perish the thought!)

## WHAT EXTRACURRICULAR INVOLVEMENT CAN TEACH YOU

It won't always be the case that your academic obligations will hinder your pursuit of serious extracurricular interest (or in the rare case, vice versa). Often the relationship will be complementary or even mutually enhancing. Before trying to say exactly what this might mean, let's look at some situations.

### Some Experiences to Learn From

You come to college a much-respected field hockey goalkeeper. Three things discourage you about your prospects right away: The infirmary is so disorganized during orientation week that you can't get your physical exam on time to participate in the first two practice sessions, your equipment is old and doesn't fit the way it should for you to feel comfortable in the goal, and the coach is paying more attention to the other freshman goalie. After two weeks, it's clear that you will be the backup junior varsity goalie for the rest of the season. It is all very discouraging for you, and you want to talk to the coach now, before the season is too far along. What do you say?

In April of your freshman year, having been elected to the editorial board of the literary magazine, you begin work with your colleagues on several basic changes in the standards and format of the magazine for the next fall. Some members of the alumni board get wind of the proposals and summon the editorial board to a meeting where it is made clear that, if the proposed changes are made, alumni funding will be withdrawn. What do you do? The alumni expect responses right there, at the meeting.

The dean, having listened for a year to complaints about

litter from the custodial staff, publishes a new policy: From now on, there will be no door-to-door dormitory delivery of leaflets or publications except magazine and newspaper subscriptions. You and the other members of the business board of the fledgling libertarian newspaper know that you need door-to-door delivery or your paper will die from lack of visibility. You are designated to call the dean for an appointment so that the business board can negotiate with him. By chance, the dean, rather than his secretary, answers the phone. What do you say over the phone? What do you say when you finally get to his office?

It is the spring of your sophomore year. Last year at about this time, you joined a century-old social club at the college. It is a much-prized membership, the best house on campus. This year, a member proposes that a Jewish freshman be invited to join. One of the reasons an invitation from the club is such a big deal is that it is made up entirely of non-Jews. You support the idea of inviting this particular freshman—you know the person and think he deserves to get in. But there is a large faction in the club, led by some strong and popular people, who say they will resign if this freshman gets a bid. How do you act on your convictions? What do you think of such exclusivity at your college, now that you are an insider? Would it make a difference if it were a year or two later and you were the chairman of the selection committee or the president of the club and felt, ex officio, responsible for preserving the organization?

A month ago, you successfully competed for a slot on the staff of the college newspaper. You've been getting pretty dull story assignments from your editor ever since. Last week, you became aware of murmurings in the dormitory next to yours and, with newly sensitive antennae, have discovered that a woman in that dorm has brought a criminal complaint of rape against another freshman. Always letting other students know you are wearing your reporter's hat, you ask questions and find out as much as the other students know, including what the young woman has to say. When you visit the president to ask about the position the college is taking in the case, the president asks you not to proceed with the story out of respect for the privacy of the two students involved. You feel you have some obligation, in a time when feelings about relations between women and men at the college are confused and being widely discussed, to get the story out. Do you honor the president's request? How do you decide where your responsibility lies?

It is the fall of your junior year. You have been a swimmer since you were in grammar school. It didn't take long after you got to college for you to realize that, no matter how hard you worked, you would never be a star. For two years now, you have gone faithfully to workouts, sometimes at 6:30 A.M., and have swum and placed in every dual meet. Halfway through your college career, you decide you want to try something else—maybe to start playing the piano again. You talk with your teammates about it and, after just a few days, the captain calls and asks to visit with you. "You can't do this," the captain says, with characteristic overstatement. "You are the sort of person that holds this team together. You are the glue. Why does everybody need to be a star? Don't relationships with teammates matter? And the team needs the depth you provide in your event." After the captain leaves, you begin to reconsider. Maybe your commitment to the team requires that you carry on until you graduate, even though it is not satisfying any more, much less fun. Is this a test of character? People who have character just don't quit.

## What Commitment Means

Situations like these come up often in college life, but when you find yourself involved in one of them, it won't matter that things like this have happened to other people. This time it's happening to you, and it's complicated. In each of these situations, authority of some kind, sometimes in the guise of conscience or tradition or other people's expectations of you, confronts you and demands that you take a position and support it with an argument—either that, or submit. It feels as though it may be stretching a point, but it isn't, to say that this is very much the situation you are in all the time in your academic work.

Such situations call for you to show your true colors. The frustration of putting in hard work for little reward calls for patience at the beginning (in part because you don't know how much better you will become in the activity) and courage and decisiveness later on. Your commitment to teammates, or colleagues in some nonathletic enterprise, calls for integrity; they depend on you to keep your promises. Confrontation with power and authority (the coach or the dean) calls on you to credit your own feelings and know your own mind.

The situations we've just discussed may be common in college life, but it isn't always so easy to see their educational value, especially at the time, or the way they can help you build toward the future. The following are even more ordinary situations that are worth looking at carefully now, so when you find yourself in similar circumstances, you can recognize their value for your political and intellectual growth.

You are sitting at a table with others. There are any number of things you can imagine yourself doing at the table:

- You and two other students have been sent by the health advisory committee of the student government to persuade the dean to install condom machines in strategic locations in the dormitories and the library.
- You are a member of the student-faculty committee assessing the quality of academic advising and recommending improvements.
- It is the end of the year and you are a member of a group that has organized an after-school tutoring and play program for a local elementary school. You are trying to gauge where you have succeeded and where you have failed in order to plan for next year.
- You are a member of the steering committee of the wilderness orientation program for freshmen, and you are trying to select group leaders for next year after spending a month interviewing 40 candidates for the 13 open slots.

You can also imagine yourself as the point person or chairman in any of these situations. How can you determine whether you know enough about the context of the discussion to participate responsibly? How will you decide what to say? Will you listen carefully enough to understand the concerns of the other participants? Once you have discovered your own position, will you want to bring other people around to it? What will you do about the wandering, the intrusions, or the sloppy thinking of others at the table? Will you be willing to leave the table without a clear sense of what the group plans to do next?

It's hard to imagine doing anything after college that won't call for the skills you can develop in such ordinary settings. If you're effective, it can be one of the most satisfying experiences you have, in part because you use so much of your talent and energy to serve purposes you share with others. At the table, you get practical training in politics and ethics. It isn't really any different from the training you get in dealing with your roommates or in some classrooms, but you can recognize it more easily.

## TRADITIONS

Colleges and universities are cloaked in tradition. It's possible that the traditions of the college will speak to you more clearly through your extracurricular involvement than through what goes on in the classroom. Traditions may show you what is unique about the college and will help you decide how you want to leave your mark on the place. There will be legendary students in old group photographs on the wall or old yearbooks in the library. By some mysterious osmosis, you will learn who they are and what they did in college and afterwards, so you can begin to get a sense of where college paths lead. Students will have their own language—names for one another, for organizations, for bureaucratic procedures, for famous courses—and that language has always been part of the college. There are ancient practices on certain spring weekends in certain locations on the campus for the initiation of new members into certain organizations. The statue of the founder comes to life under certain circumstances or endows a beholder with magical powers if a certain combination of things is said or done. The clapper from the bell announcing the change of classes each hour must be stolen at the earliest possible moment by a freshman. It is a disgrace if a sister college down (or up) the line ever wins an athletic contest between the two institutions. Students from the college have always organized a field day for the kids from town or have sent a huge float and the marching band down Main Street on St. Patrick's Day. These rituals contribute to institutional "character" you won't be able to ignore.

There may be a strong tradition of preparing for national service or leadership in business because of something the president of the college said 100 years ago. Or the religious traditions of the college support a famous symposium of faculty, students, and outside speakers on ethics once a year. The traditions of the college provide frames of reference and vocabularies for you to use in thinking through and organizing your own life in college. Sometimes traditions can be problematic. Their weight may keep you from feeling that you can contribute to change. On the other hand, a lack of tradition can make you feel like a passenger on a rudderless ship. And, after you've been at the college for a little while, you may even feel that its traditions are so alien to your own that you can never be part of them. But you should believe that any work you do in making a place and a name for yourself there can reshape the traditions of the college—although you may not see how until you can look back.

## PARTIES

One tradition you are probably already anticipating is college socializing-"partying," as it is called. Parties, like everything else in college life, come in many shapes and sizes—including cast parties, athletic teams celebrating the end of a season, faculty teas, gatherings of students and alumni, holiday parties, and picnics and barbecues sponsored by the college. None of those events is the real thing, however, in the college vernacular; a real party centers on several kegs of beer wrapped in layers of deafening music.

You may not be comfortable, though, with the "work hard, play hard" ethic.

> *I see an amazing number of people pushing themselves like mad all week and then releasing all this tension on the*

> weekends by partying with the same intensity. For me,
> meaningful friendships have been hard to come by in this
> atmosphere.

In the early weeks, you may feel that there are only two options available to you in connection with college parties—to go to them or to stay away from them—but, either way, you must put up with endless talk about them. In fact, there are many other satisfactory alternatives. There is no rule on the books against reformulating the notion of college parties, although it may take an effort to see the possibilities that are comfortable for you.

> *I am not the right person to talk about social life, because I have had some rough times. Basically, I am not a social being. Don't get me wrong—I love people, but only one or two or four at a time, not a lot. Although I have tried, unsuccessfully and with depressing results, to convince myself that I should love large parties and dances, I found out that I really don't. But there is something here for everyone. I love to sit with a couple of friends and talk about everything possible. This I have done and enjoyed. I love to play pinball and have met some dear friends over the machines. So when I have fun here with a few friends, I really have fun!*

You can ask questions about large alcohol-centric parties in the same way you ask about other extracurricular activities—whether, for example, they are occasions that make people happy, that discover or develop friendships, that provide a change of pace from the anxiety of course work and exams, and so forth—or simply try to discover what relationship they have to the rest of college experience. You may find, on reflection, that they are none of these things, but sheer, wild release from the academic grind. People sometimes admit they go to such parties not to find their friends or to dance, but to get drunk. Unfortunately, often the aftermath of the event is people being violently ill or just plain violent. Such a party is poised on the edge of outlawry, because state laws and college rules are about to be violated, and on the edge of chaos, because someone is about to be sick or injured or property is about to be damaged.

You may find that you and your friends prefer different kinds of parties, ones at which there is less liquor, you can talk and dance and get caught up with people you know, and people will depart happy and sober. On the other hand, you may find that your friends prefer a keg and that you are sometimes a host at this more "traditional" kind of party. Think about what such events are good for and what contribution you want to make to them. Once again, finding a balance is essential.

> *I guess this is the place to talk about the scheduling of time between academics and social life. Frankly, that is the hardest part of freshman year. Suddenly we are independent souls who must apportion our own time. It is very tempting to put off everything until reading period and then cram for finals. I somehow managed to escape that fate, but I don't know my secret. I watched people all around me panicking over work they hadn't done. On the other hand, there are people who do nothing but work and consequently have virtually no social life whatsoever. Somewhere there must be a happy medium—a balance between work and play. I wish luck to those who search for that balance.*

*My attitude towards him is an attitude towards a soul.*
(Wittgenstein)

*There are few even whom I should venture to call earnestly by their most proper names. A name pronounced is the recognition of the individual to whom it belongs. He who can pronounce my name aright, he can call me, and is entitled to my love and service.*
(Thoreau)

# 12
# Keeping Your Mind Open

Colleges are generally more diverse than high schools because they can draw students and faculty from a wider world. Even if your college turns out to be less diverse than your high school—if, for example, your journey is from a very large, urban high school to a small, homogeneous regional college in a rural town whose main business is the college—you will find yourself in an unfamiliar situation at first. You may have to learn some essential lessons all over again to get on in this new setting. You may have to use some skills that threaten to become rusty with disuse.

> *Socially, I cannot say I am fully satisfied with this year. Coming from a very close-knit family and a small community, I found the lack of interest and general coolness on the part of many people here particularly disturbing. Perhaps I am being unfair, however. I must admit that in my insecurity here, at times I have tended to crawl back into my shell and not attempt to relate to other people. I suppose that any inadequacies that I see in my social life here are to be blamed on myself, rather than on the community.*

## REACTING TO DIFFERENCES

In the early weeks and months in college, your most powerful experiences may be of differences: your differences from others, theirs from you, theirs from one another. Regional differences may strike you first: people in this part of the country are unfriendly and too busy, or they talk too slowly and are hypocritically friendly, or they don't take anything seriously, or they are not sophisticated. But even beyond these apparent differences, when you meet your roommates for the first time, when you enter the freshman dining hall for the first time, when you sit in your first lecture, or when you go to an orientation meeting of the newspaper, you will collect impressions. You'd like to be as self-confident as this person. This other person acts as though he and his family own the college. This one is just too black for you to be comfortable with, that one dresses beautifully, this one may be gay, that one's accent is so thick you wonder whether she is qualified for college. Because you are new to the place, and the variety of people is greater than you are used to, you begin to see black, white, Asian, Hispanic, private-school, public-school, liberal, conservative, middle-of-the-road, Italian, Irish, Arab, Jew, Catholic, female, male, gay, straight, athlete, nonathlete, rich, poor, old-college, noncollege, even old and young, where at home you simply saw people you knew. Your new world can be populated by categories rather than people. It's easy to describe your circle of acquaintances in these terms:

> *Aside from one preppie and one premed upstairs, our entry had a good group.*

You may recognize and even relish individual differences as important ingredients in an exciting educational process. On the other hand, you can begin to think in categories. Ironically, the college itself seems to invite this way of thinking.

## Generalizing

The admissions committee ensures that the college stays diverse by asking applicants to identify themselves by race or ethnic group. But one consequence of having to check a box on an application is that some students come to college thinking they were admitted only because of some government pressure on the college for affirmative action, and so they are ready to believe that their college has special standards or even quotas for certain racial or ethnic groups. An even more insidious effect, for example, is that on the black student who convinces himself he is at the college only because he is black and assumes that the college therefore doesn't have high academic expectations of him. He may persuade himself bitterly that there is no need to work very hard or to try to measure up to his considerable potential. If pressed, white students will sometimes admit that they think many minority students are at the college because of some sort of affirmative action program and therefore may not really be qualified. Minority students resent that attitude but can also convince themselves that the majority is right.

Thinking categorically about others or about oneself can have subtly harmful effects in almost every area of college life. Sometimes it isn't very easy to see that racism or sexism or homophobia is waiting to flower. At other times, what is lurking in a situation is perfectly clear.

The following stories are enough like real episodes from college life for you to see them as representative. They are not all stories of racism (people of color victimized by whites, for example), sexism (women victimized by men and vice versa), or homophobia (gays victimized by straights). But they are all stories in which people fail to treat other people—or themselves—as individuals. As you read, try to see yourself as one or more of the characters in each story.

There is a table in the freshman dining hall where some of the black students sit at every meal. A white student will occasionally sit down with the group. That works fine; the group is not exclusive, and students who are not black are always made to feel welcome. Black students who are not comfortable sitting at the table, for whatever reason, are a different story. They are subtly made to feel as though they are not black enough, as though they have an obligation to sit there, as though they are somehow betraying their race if they don't. Encouraging new students to sit at this table is the way the Black Student Organization reaches out to freshmen.

Such an arrangement can allow people to explore and affirm their racial identities, which is a good thing. It can also be an exclusive place where people feel a great deal of pressure to express their membership in a group in approved ways, which is not a good thing and can be alienating, divisive, and embittering. How do you sort out your own attitudes toward the table?

## Stereotypes

Wallace has come to college from a small parochial school in a large city 100 miles from the college. He is a Chinese American. His family is important to him, and he worries about them all the time. His father, the owner of a small business, is not doing well financially, his parents' marriage is strained, and his younger sister, always rebelling in some dramatic way, has a troubled relationship with their parents. Wallace is also especially sensitive to the stereotype of the Asian college student, which he sees as academically oriented, earning high grades in math and science, coping with high expectations on the part of parents for success in college and for a career in medicine—what Wallace calls "the Asian premed nerd." Wallace worries all the time that he will live up to the stereotype, a caricature he cannot stand, and so he puts a great deal of energy into not doing so. He doesn't have much money, but the little he has he invests in clothes: turtlenecks, timbies, topsiders, and other gear from acceptable outdoor outfitters. He becomes Super Prep. He does almost no work. He also tries to be very cool about his troubled family, as though having a troubled family is a status symbol. In his effort to avoid one stereotype, he falls into another and refuses to admit, even to himself, that he worries about how things are at home.

Sometimes students neglect themselves under pressure to be seen in a certain way. Talents and deep, long-term interests can be left by the wayside, leading to potentially disastrous consequences. On the other hand, many people do try on new personas from time to time in life and feel free to see themselves as they are or genuinely want to be. How do you avoid being trapped inside a new identity?

## Clichés

Vic meets Grace at a party one Saturday night. She is pretty and very funny. They have a wonderful time together and get quite drunk. They walk back to her dormitory room together and she invites him in to talk. They lie down on the bed after a little while, still feeling the effects of the beer, and begin to kiss. Vic decides he wants to do more than that and presses Grace to have intercourse with him. She says no several times but doesn't push him away. Vic decides that she doesn't really mean she doesn't want to do it and that girls always put up some resistance—it's part of the game. So he presses on and achieves his objective. Afterward, Grace cries and asks him to leave, which he does, knowing that crying afterward is also what girls do. A week later, he is summoned by the dean, who tells him that Grace has made a formal complaint of rape to the sexual harassment hearing officer and the disciplinary committee.

It may be alcohol that convinces Vic that he knows what "girls" always do. On the other hand, he may always have hung out with friends to whom women were not real people; the beer just inspires him to act on the conviction. Vic confuses this opportunity for sex with the right to have sex in spite of Grace's objections. Because she isn't real for him, he feels free to hurt her. Listen to your own talk about the opposite sex—how does it sound?

## Responsibility

One morning after he and his friends have finished breakfast in the dining hall, Derek decides to take a loaf of bread from the toast table. He puts it under his baseball jacket and walks out the front door. Just as he gets outside, he is called back by the dining-hall manager, who quietly takes him aside, tells him to return the bread, requests his ID number, and says she is going to report him to the dean. In his meeting with the dean that afternoon, Derek says that everybody takes food from the dining hall; in fact, he had seen another person taking some fruit after breakfast that very morning without getting stopped. The dining-hall manager has a reputation as a racist, he says, and she stopped him only because he is black.

Derek uses his race as a defensive weapon here: trying to keep the dean at bay, accusing the dining-hall manager, and avoiding responsibility. The terms of his argument need to be challenged consistently. It may be that the dining-hall manager is racist, but Derek must still account for his actions. Under what circumstances is racism an explanation?

## Respect

Late one afternoon, passersby outside a dormitory known to have a heavy concentration of male athletes are surprised to see the torso of a female clothing-store manikin hanging from a second-floor window. It is grotesquely painted to emphasize certain portions of the female anatomy and attached to an obscene sign that is derogatory toward women. Several women, known to other students as radical feminists, complain to the president of the college about this display, and the men who live in the room are brought before the judicial board. They protest that they were only joking and didn't think it would offend anyone. The board puts them on probation for a year and prohibits them from participating in their sports. The student body is deeply divided over the incident, which is discussed for weeks in the campus paper.

What's the real issue here? Overreaction to a joke—by a group of politically active women? Freedom of expression? Perhaps we ought to be thinking about the care and respect that a community requires for its day-to-day survival and the care and respect that any woman passing that dormitory deserves. Are there other issues?

## Prejudice of Others

Byron is a frail, wispy-haired, bespectacled freshman with a bad complexion who seems to spend most of his time in the terminal room or at his own PC, playing computer games or doing his computer science problem sets. He is teased gently by his more robust roommates, who have other interests, and is occasionally treated by them as though he doesn't exist—until they discover, one day in October as they read the sports pages of the student newspaper over lunch, that Byron is a champion distance runner who is expected by the track coach to be a standout in college. The roommates do a turnaround, and Byron suddenly finds himself popular.

Why is Byron a different person once he is discovered to have athletic talent? How can the same person be an ignored geek one day and a revered jock the next?

## Identity

One day the dean is disturbed by the sounds of protest outside his office window. He looks out and sees a group of about 50 minority students picketing the building, carrying signs and listening to a speaker denouncing the administration for refusing to establish special orientation programs for minority freshmen. The dean goes out to respond to the complaints and to receive a list of demands, and after half an hour the protesters disband. One stays behind, and the dean recognizes him as a young man named Dwight whose adviser had several weeks earlier described him to the dean as tortured by the question of whether he is black or white, since his father is black and his mother white. The dean invites Dwight into his office, where Dwight tells him that the reason the dean has these political problems is that he doesn't understand the black perspective. Dwight does understand it, he tells the dean, and has brought a book that may help him. He hands the dean a worn paperback copy of a book called *Black Like Me*. The dean remembers that the book, which was published in the mid-1950s, is a first-person account of a white journalist who disguises himself as a black man and goes into the deep South to discover the experiences of blacks for himself.

How will Dwight find room to be himself in a college where political battle lines are sometimes drawn in racial terms? Are fellow students going to press him to decide whether he is black or white? Or will they just leave him alone?

## Sexual Orientation

Warren has known for a year that he is gay. By the time he arrives at college, he is relatively comfortable with this knowledge but doesn't know how his roommates will feel about it. He waits until mid-November before saying anything to them. Of the two, Kareem seems the more deeply troubled by the news; Peter doesn't even acknowledge that he has heard what Warren said. Kareem says that he is very disturbed, and that he isn't sure whether he can live with Warren and plans to take the issue up with their assistant dean. Warren never hears how that meeting goes, or even if it has taken place, but he does begin to feel that Kareem is involving Peter in a campaign of harassment. For weeks, every night after he goes to bed, Warren can hear the two talking about him in the other room, calling him names and wondering out loud what his sexual experiences have been like. He is worried and even slightly scared, because he thinks he has heard them planning to attack him. He confronts his roommates, but they deny having these conversations, so he goes to the dean for help.

Since it's possible that you will be assigned to live with someone who is gay, do you know how you will react? If you already react to the prospect with fear and disgust, do you know what those feelings are based on? What if you like and respect your roommate before the announcement—what difference will this new information make? Is there anyone you can talk with about this? If you are gay, are there some ways of letting roommates know that are better than other ways? Can anyone help you find out?

## Self-Image

Nick comes to college with a pretty good high school career as a running back. The college coach had even written to him a couple of times. By the end of his freshman season, though, it is clear that Nick is not going to be invited to preseason camp in his sophomore year. For five years, maybe even since junior high, he has thought of himself as a jock. He doesn't see what he is going to do and who he is going to be once he no longer has afternoon practices. He is so preoccupied with these thoughts that during the spring semester of his freshman year, he never says a word in class.

Do you dismiss Nick as only a jock? Why? You might find yourself in Nick's situation someday. Is there something you can do now to avoid being silent all spring?

## Assumptions

Darla is taking a philosophy course whose topic is justice. She is one of two women in a class of 12. From the beginning, she notices that the instructor, who is male, rarely calls on her even if she volunteers. But it isn't until he turns to her one day during a discussion of abortion and asks her for the feminine point of view on the question of whether the fetus is a person that she feels insulted and angry.

This instructor may think he is doing just the right thing to enrich discussion. Is he? If you were a member of the class, what might you say after hearing his question? How might Darla express her feelings? Or shouldn't she? Should she just let it slide?

## **EMPATHY**

In order to find alternatives to the way people in these stories see others, or assume others see them, it might be worth imagining what it must be like to be someone else. It's hard to do this under most circumstances, but starting out new at something can make it even more difficult. Everybody needs categories and labels in order to get started. In the first months at college, there is so much that needs to be learned right away that people will seize any opportunity to sum something up, put it somewhere safe, and move on to the next something. "There," you say, "I've got that figured out—what's next?" This way of getting from one moment to the next may be especially tempting when you are confronted with a rainbow of individuals so colorful you can't see how you will ever be able to take them all in. So you begin systematically to pigeonhole most of the people you encounter, to protect yourself from being overwhelmed. And college lingo provides a veritable filing system with which to store people until you are ready for them: geek, prep, nerd, groid, dweeb, jock, jap, fag, creepoid, wimp, honkie, loser, motor head, hick, and on and on.

You probably will have said in your application for admission and in your interviews with local alumni and admissions staff that part of what pulls you toward college in general and their college in particular is the possibility of learning from people who are different from you. But it won't take long to learn that actually living with that variety and growing because of it, rather than talking about it theoretically, takes work. It requires looking, listening, trying to figure out what it must be like to be in that person's skin (whatever color or complexion), comparing the perspective you ascribe to that person with your own, making room for other people's peculiarities, slowly and carefully increasing your understanding of the ways other people look at the world.

The following can be typical of a rooming group.

> *Despite the crowded conditions, I really enjoyed the people I was assigned to live with. Obviously, an interest in politics and international relations united us. The group included a Liberian black Third World defender, a Swedish socialist, a Long Island Jewish intellectual, a Southern reactionary (ah, I reveal my bias!), and an American whose family has lived in 11 different countries. I was assigned the role of Eastern establishment WASP in this group. And although our backgrounds were all very different and our views rarely converged, we debated morality, life, and politics long into the night on many occasions. I was forced to question my own values, reevaluate them, and defend them like I never had before. Undoubtedly, I learned more from this than from anything else at college.*

## Learning from Differences

Taking advantage of diversity is different from exclaiming to people back home how diverse your college is or assuming complacently that your education will automatically be richer because of this diversity. Learning from diversity will involve taking some risks—exposing yourself in ways that may make you vulnerable to criticism from people you consider your friends and swimming against some strong social currents. The motive for taking risks will probably have to be something closer to the bone than an abstract ideal—of tolerance, for example, a notion too passive to accomplish much in the way of education, anyway. Your motive will probably be that it is, for reasons of your own and no one else's, worthwhile to discover in other people all that makes them colorful and ordinary, kind and mean, generous and stingy, brave and cowardly—even though the effort you must make in the face of resistance or even scorn may cause you pain.

Thinking about these things may wake familiar echoes in you; why, after all, should ways of thinking about respecting others in a college community be different from ways of thinking about the intellectual tasks in college courses? Both enterprises call for curiosity, risk, imagination, compassion, and judgment.

## COLLEGE AS "OPPORTUNITY"

If you value diversity but don't think critically about it, you can become dangerously complacent about what a wonderful opportunity college represents.

> *This college plucked me out of a small, secluded, poor Puerto Rican community in Trenton, New Jersey and threw me into this totally new environment and expected me to adjust. HA! The first few weeks I met people, became aware of my ignorance in many fields, felt intimidated because of my weak educational background, and felt "different." After about a month here, I came so close to quitting that I can't describe it. Let me tell you, life was hard on me, and I did not want to deal with it. No one showed enough interest to support or console me; the only way I hung in there was with the help of God, my mother's prayers, and a lot of unnecessary suffering. I cried, and still do. Everything should not be this way. I hate racism.*

You may come from a background that has not prepared you to fall in easily with the long tradition of the college. For example, you may be a person of color coming to a college that was almost completely white until 15 years ago, or a woman at a college that had no women until the early seventies, or the first member of a blue-collar family to go to college who feels as though every collar ever worn at your college has been high, white, and starched. All the portraits hanging in the main reading room of the library are of people who could not have been your ancestors or of people you feel you cannot grow up to be. In these circumstances, you may feel from time to time as though you have been brought to the college in order to teach everyone else there something about your tradition or culture—and you may resent it. You may feel as though you are being asked to do all the reaching out and the educating, as though the people from more traditional backgrounds can sit on their hands and wait for you to make the first move. You may feel that you are not only bearing the considerable burden of being alien but that of having to educate others as well.

If you are a member of the majority in your college and think of yourself as a "liberal," you may resent the banding together of minority students. Why do they always sit together in the dining hall? Why do they have such active and vocal organizations? Why is there a Third World Center? Why can't they all just become part of the larger community? As a first step toward answering the questions (but only a first step), you might look around and see where the members of the hockey team live and where the graduates of the St. Grottlesex School eat.

## **TRADITIONS, GROUPS, AND INDIVIDUALS**

The existence of supportive subcommunities is essential to the survival of individuals, especially in college, where the atmosphere can be impersonal and the traditions alien. But look at the actual function of such groups and the behavior of individuals in them. The group may become so comfortable, compared to the more chaotic and risky world of the college at large, that you never quite work up the energy to reach out beyond the group—this can be true even if the group is very active and politically vocal. On the other hand, the group may not be especially comfortable for you, but it may be the only place you can begin to learn about your own racial or ethnic tradition, since you come from a school and a community that have made that impossible. What is to be done about all this?

Avoiding groupthink may be as easy or as hard as simply not relegating yourself to a category. I am not only an athlete, you might say to yourself; last year I had a major part in the drama festival play back home. I am not only a Chicano from East L.A.; I won a poetry prize and play a mean game of chess.

These acknowledgments and proclamations are personal and are made by inner voices before they are heard by anyone else, but they point to something precious: your own unique diversity. Preserving and enhancing that will ultimately be more important than contributing to and benefiting from the cultural and intellectual diversity of the college, though finally you won't be able to accomplish one without working at the other as well.

Assimilation is a comfortable ideal if you are a member of the majority tradition of your college; it will probably be relatively easy for you to internalize school values and become absorbed by them—if that is what you want to do. If you come to the college from another tradition, you may not be interested in assimilating at all, even though resisting the pressures in that direction may be be quite uncomfortable. You may, in fact, find yourself wanting to use the resources of the college—people, books, and perspective—to learn about your own tradition so that you know as much as anybody else does about where you are coming from when the topic is music or politics or the transformation of the modern family.

This idea, of teaching yourself as much about your own tradition as you can, may help us see something about the sort of community a college can be at its best—not thinking of itself as a melting pot nor taking assimilation as its goal. Perhaps the ideal is individuals or small groups working together to understand as much as possible about the traditions represented in order to discover what values are held in common and what values cannot, and therefore will not, be held in common. The vision described would be a college "community" filled not just with heat but with light as well, and worthy of the name.

So when Guy persuades the other members of the black table to publish a political and literary magazine whose purpose is to express the individual perspectives black students have on their experiences, he is doing a service to the college as a whole. And Judith's efforts may do something to enhance a sense of real community when she and three other people from the freshman council sponsor a series of special Sunday night suppers in the dining hall, featuring Italian, Cajun, Irish, Jewish, Mexican, and soul food. And Dean Forthcoming may be doing something substantial along the same lines when she establishes a race-relations advisory committee comprising students, staff, and faculty of almost as many colors and traditions as there are in the college.

## Understanding Is the Goal

There is at least one more thing to say about categorical thinking. We need categories in order to understand any similarities and differences that are worth working with (this chapter itself depends on categories, after all), but the categories should serve as only a first step toward understanding. When categories become stereotypes (inflexible caricatures), they become ends rather than means. Stereotyping is a radical, unimaginative way of putting others at a safe distance or dismissing them altogether. A stereotype is a category that has become an intellectual and spiritual trap. Behavior based on stereotyping can become racist or sexist or homophobic. Examine your own assumptions about people to see whether they are justified by your experience just as you would examine your assumptions when you want to make an intellectual argument that someone else will respect.

If you are in a room of three—one white, one black, and one Asian—and you begin to suspect that the Asian, who is under tremendous pressure from her family to perform well academically, is stealing from you—food at first, then clothing, and now small sums of money—what importance will her race have in your decision about voicing your suspicions? If you discover that your roommate is gay and you are nervous and even frightened about this, will you assume that you have only two courses of action: the "bleeding-heart-liberal" response, which you assume is to accept all differences in silence, or the "redneck" response, which is to warn him about his behavior by beating him up? Will college life convince you, because of attention paid to categories in the press, in class, and in committees of various sorts, that the facts of your being a woman and Hispanic will determine everything that happens to you and that individuality will count for nothing?

A black student comes to the dean to urge him not to establish special orientation programs for minority freshmen—even though both the student and the dean see that such programs might go a long way to show minority students they belong at the college and can even own a part of it. The student recently had a disturbing experience. He is a senior and has been granted interviews by several medical schools. At three of the schools, he says, he has had to meet with a subcommittee of the faculty admission committee, a group of minority medical students who have taken it upon themselves to discover, among other things, the strength of the candidate's commitment to returning to his community to serve his people. What disturbs this student is that there seems to be no allowance for his interests in research and teaching. He has come to urge the dean not to support special programs, because such support might help perpetuate in certain academic procedures, like admissions, forms of categorical thinking that are unhealthy—for everybody.

The challenge delivered to every student in a college that is diverse with respect to class, race, ethnicity, politics, and sexual orientation is how to respect individuality while acknowledging the need almost everyone has to associate in groups whose members are familiar to one another and even like-minded on some issues. It is asking too much to expect people to allow themselves to be taken exclusively as individuals and to set aside their blackness or their gayness, their femaleness or their maleness.

What are the applications of all this discussion of categories, labels, stereotypes, and individuals for everyday college life? Stay open and curious about the details of other people's lives—their ideas, their tastes, their adventures small and large, their families' attitudes toward what they are doing, the history of their families, the nature of their home towns and neighborhoods, the feel of their homes, their religion, their politics (even their racial or sexual politics). Ask and listen. Answer and talk.

Calling another person (even silently) a nigger, faggot, white boy, jock, or girl means that you are dismissing or excluding that person, turning your back on him or her, consigning a person to a bin containing all others of that sort. Calling another person by a given name or even, after a time, by a nickname you both have agreed will be the person's special name between you distinguishes that person from all others and is an invitation to a conversation. Talk to me, you seem to say. I am facing you. I am open to you. I will listen to you. I need to know you and your tradition for your sake and my own.

*And who is my neighbour?*

(Luke 10:29)

# 13
## *Becoming Entangled*

As we saw in Chapter 11, the extracurricular distractions in college are many. The challenge in such a world is not to be led too far from your purposes in being there and not to let things get too far off balance for too long. Sometimes a distraction can take a form that is even subtler in its appeal than a sport or the newspaper or your music or computer hacking. It can promise comfort or security or control or temporary release from pain and thus be so important that you become almost obsessed.

This chapter is therefore not only an exploration of challenges of a particular kind but also a description of some representative situations in which self-awareness and good judgment will be particularly important. Involvement with drugs or alcohol or with another person in a sexual relationship can clearly lead to such situations. But there are other types of involvement as well that can take you as far away from your educational pursuits.

Let's begin this chapter with stories. Try to see yourself both as the main character in each and as a roommate or friend. If you find it hard to conceive of yourself as getting into one of these situations, you may find it easier to imagine it of someone who is reasonably close to you and for whom you feel some responsibility. Everyone who becomes entangled in one of these situations is someone's friend or roommate.

## **LETTING GO OF THE PAST**

Cyril comes to college from a large, academically demanding urban high school where he has worked reasonably hard to achieve a good record. He has chosen to enroll in a university in the same city in part because his parents separated during his senior year and asked him not to go too far away. He skipped a grade in elementary school and is a year younger than most of his classmates. Cyril was not very involved in activities outside of class in high school, but he has lots of friends, many of whom are a year behind him. He and his friends spent the year before Cyril graduated having parties at one another's houses, at which they always drank wine and smoked marijuana. He has enjoyed his reputation as a sophisticated druggie.

When Cyril gets to college, he feels awkward because the other students in his dormitory seem so much more at ease and ready for the demands of college life. They all seem to know exactly what they want to study and what else they want to do, while he doesn't have any real interests. They drink beer, but they don't smoke. So Cyril takes to inviting his high school friends to the dormitory on weekends in order not to lose the kind of socializing he was so comfortable with in high school. His friends mean a great deal to him. He misses them during the week, and he feels happy only when they are around. He introduces them to his dormmates but makes no effort otherwise to include the people in the dormitory in his circle of friends. Cyril depends on these weekends with his friends from high school. So although he has many acquaintances, he makes no friends in college. It's all right with the other people in his dormitory if he wants to be a loner during the week, but they resent his friends' taking over the entry on weekends. Cyril involves himself in nothing other than his courses and his weekends and eventually begins to let his courses slide. He never feels right unless he is with his old friends, drinking and smoking. Once, he invites a larger number of old friends than usual to the dormitory on a Saturday night. Several of them get out of hand and trash a bathroom and the stairwell of the entry. The RA is called, and Cyril finds himself facing college discipline because, by the college's rules, he is responsible for the conduct of his guests. His dormmates are losing patience with him.

The partying cools down a bit, but at the end of the first semester Cyril's academic record is unsatisfactory, and he is asked to talk with the dean. The conversation goes pretty well. He uses some of his high school debate skills and manages to avoid probation. The dean asks about his social life, but Cyril puts up smoke screens. By the end of the second semester, though he has no more discipline problems, his record has not improved, so he is required by the committee that reviews unsatisfactory grades to leave college for a year. At this point, in the aftermath of this decision, he is able to admit to his adviser and his parents that his social life, his drinking, and his drug use are habits that stem from fear of his own awkwardness and that his lack of intellectual motivation and academic direction comes from his terror of academic failure. Most important, he can say that his parents' divorce has made him reluctant to risk real friendships.

How do you react to the story of Cyril's first year in college? Is he afraid to fail? It's clear he never quite lets go of high school or really comes to college. Probably nobody quite lets go or really gets there by the end of freshman year, so everybody has some of Cyril in him or her. On the other hand, Cyril's story is unusual because his involvement with his old friends doesn't change much once he gets to college and seems to keep him from even getting to know the people in his new world and from applying himself academically. Just as striking and important is Cyril's reluctance to let go of familiar, secure habits and patterns: the wine and the marijuana and the social activities they sustain. His attempt to bring his old world wholesale into the new fails when his friends, who have no reason to treat the dormitory or its occupants with any consideration, finally spin out from under Cyril's not-so-firm control. They seem to be taking advantage of him, perhaps because his dorm is freer than their homes. But so long as Cyril can depend on old friends for company and entertainment, he has no motivation to decide what he wants from his time in college, and everything seems to sink down with him into a day-to-day depression. He can see no reason to stay in college and, in fact, because of his academic failure, a committee requires him to leave.

## MEETING NEW TEMPTATIONS

One Saturday evening in November of her freshman year, when most of her class has left campus for the weekend, Rena sits down alone to have supper in the dining hall. A young woman carrying a supper tray approaches Rena's table and asks if she can join her. Rena says yes, and the woman, who introduces herself only as Carolyn, begins chatting in the easiest, most natural sort of way, asking Rena about particular recent events in the college and wondering aloud where particular people might have gone for the weekend. Though Rena can't remember having seen Carolyn before, she assumes it is because she is a freshman and it is only November, and she soon finds herself having the most enjoyable conversation she has had since leaving home two months earlier. Shortly, she is confiding to Carolyn that although she enjoys her courses and is doing quite well, she's had a very hard time making friends. Her sophisticated classmates make her feel unsure about her own abilities and whether she belongs, and she misses the spiritual support of family, friends, and church back home in North Carolina.

Over tea, after they've been sitting together for more than an hour, Carolyn asks Rena if she'd like to come with her to her church fellowship meeting the next evening. The invitation touches Rena. She thinks it's very kind of Carolyn, and suddenly she wants desperately to meet some people who might fill the empty places in her life. So Rena agrees to meet Carolyn at the front gate of the campus Sunday evening and go to fellowship with her.

Early Sunday evening, a battered station wagon pulls up to the gate. Rena has been waiting for about 20 minutes. Carolyn introduces her to Garth, who is driving, and Stephen. Both young men are friendly and funny, and Rena feels quite comfortable with them. The four set off together and drive for half an hour. Rena finds herself two towns away, being introduced at a meeting, not in a church, as she expected, but in the warm living room of a luxurious private home.

There are about 20 people in the room, welcoming Rena warmly and expressing lively interest in her. When the meeting starts, Carolyn introduces Rena formally and describes their meeting in the college dining hall. She says how sad and lonely Rena seemed to her, and how much she wanted Rena to meet the members of the fellowship. When it is Rena's turn to speak, she admits how lonely she has been. She finds the group so sympathetic that she goes on talking, telling about her first months at college and how hard they have been. Very soon Rena is crying and saying how grateful she is for the kindness of the fellowship. The people in the room gather around her, murmuring sympathetically; they begin to hug her and say they will take care of her, become her friends, take the place of her family while she is away from home, and be her community for as long as she needs them. Rena feels surrounded by their warmth and their love and asks how she can become a member of the group. Finally, she thinks, someone acts as though I am important and worth taking care of.

The fellowship is part of the Beaconsfield Church of the Master. Rena's group is one of 10 in the immediate area of the college. No one else in the group, not Carolyn or Garth or Stephen, is a student at the college. They meet four evenings each week and study the Bible at every meeting, memorizing long passages and hearing from the leader of the fellowship, a powerful and charming man known as the Teacher, exactly what the passages mean. To earn full membership, after two months, Rena is working several hours a week in her gentle but persuasive way to recruit new members for the fellowship from her college and from a community college in the next town. She fears that if she doesn't produce members, her new friends will withdraw their love from her. She has seen one other member of the group shunned and is terrified that the same might happen to her.

Meanwhile, she does almost no academic work. She does nothing extracurricular either and makes no friends at the college. There is no time for anything but her work for the church. At the end of the fall term, her grades are barely satisfactory; by the middle of spring semester, she is failing every course. Her RA and the assistant dean ask her about what is going on in her life, but she only reassures them vaguely and says that everything is under control and will turn out all right. At the end of the spring term, she is just getting by academically and is considering giving up math, which she has always loved, to major in religion. (Religion seems "right" now, because of her involvement in the church.)

Do you see what has happened to Rena? A member of a group whose methods are extremely sophisticated approaches her at a time and place at which she is alone and vulnerable, an away weekend in the freshman dining hall; takes advantage of her vulnerability, her homesickness, and her longing for family and church; and substitutes herself and her group's ambitions for Rena's college community and the academic ambitions that drew her there. For many weeks, Rena feels so loved and protected in that fellowship that she cannot pay attention to the concern expressed by her advisers. It isn't until she begins to see how far away the possibility of completing her education is receding, how much control the fellowship exerts over how its members read the Bible, and how it perpetuates and enlarges the group by constant, enforced recruitment efforts by every member that she eventually is able to break away, with help from people at the college and at home.

## COPING IN INAPPROPRIATE WAYS

Truman, a lacrosse player from Florida, is selected by *Lacrosse Illustrated* to its All-America second team at the end of the summer before his senior year in high school. In his senior year, he is heavily recruited by six colleges with strong lacrosse programs, is admitted to all of them, and finally chooses to attend an academically rigorous university in the Northeast. There, Truman rooms with two people who share his intense interest in sports, a tight end from Massachusetts and an outfielder from Michigan. He thinks they are great people, and he is right, but all three begin to contribute to a mutual problem when they become the nucleus of a large group of freshman athletes who spend a lot of time together and with nobody else, socializing and working out in the weight room when their sports are not in practice. In the second week of fall practice in early November, Truman breaks his leg.

Forced into near immobility by a cast that reaches almost to his hip and having to make his way everywhere on crutches, Truman begins to put on weight. By January, he has gained 20 pounds, done very little academic work, and spent every weekend carousing with one group or another of his athletic buddies. He is warned by the dean about his grades at midyear.

One Saturday night in late March, when it has been unseasonably warm, he and a group of friends come out of a dormitory after having consumed the better part of a keg of beer during the previous three hours and make their way, by fits and starts, across the quadrangle. From the porch of a nearby dorm, out of the shadows, comes a not very politely phrased request to quiet down. Truman walks toward the voice and invites the owner of it to come forward and repeat the request. The invitation is accepted, and after about three minutes, the events of which never do get sorted out perfectly in the investigation that begins on Monday morning, Truman has broken the nose of a visitor from another college.

In the course of looking into the Saturday night incident, the dean learns from Truman and his companions that Truman has been drunk to the point of passing out every weekend since breaking his leg. His friends have covered for him with the RA and have never taken him to the infirmary. Truman is allowed by the discipline committee to stay in college on probation because there is some merit to his claim that he was provoked into fighting. He promises the dean that he will curb his drinking. Two months later, he is discovered at 4 A.M., drunk to incoherence and hammering on the locked door of a dormitory not his own, demanding to be let in. In the aftermath of this incident, the dean discovers that Truman's uncle and grandfather were alcoholics.

Truman's story suggests that he sees himself first and foremost, maybe even exclusively, as a jock. When he can't be a jock he is in real trouble. He chooses to hang around only with athletes, almost from the moment he arrives at college. None of them seems to be able to separate himself from the group even to suggest that there might be other ways of getting to know their classmates or having a social life. Truman knows he is the nephew and grandson of alcoholics; in fact, deep inside he worried about that as he headed off to college, since he had been in minor difficulty three times in high school, and he knew how easy it would be to depend on alcohol in college to make socializing with new people a little easier. What do you suppose his roommates and friends think they are protecting him from and why? Understandably, they don't distinguish very well between illness and misconduct. But someone with an alcohol problem will get help from the college. Irresponsible behavior will call for disciplinary action, which may mean that help and discipline will both be part of a complex reaction on the part of the college; but drinking, by itself, will not be the occasion for punishment, unless the college has said up front that it will be.

## COMPULSIONS

Leslie toys with her food. Her roommates notice it the first time they all eat supper together but think that she isn't hungry because it is freshman week and she is excited and distracted or that she isn't feeling well and doesn't want to say so. But they soon realize that she always toys with her food and eats almost nothing, even though she takes large portions from the serving tables. Leslie also talks about food when she talks about anything. After the rush and activity of orientation week, when everybody is forced to be sociable, she seems to withdraw and always to be quite tense. Soon her roommates leave her pretty much alone and, after about a month at school, Leslie eats by herself in a remote corner of the back dining room.

Her roommates, and the very small number of friends who are patient with her solitary ways, know she was a distance runner in high school, a stellar runner in fact, and that she is running varsity cross country, one of two freshmen to make the team. What they don't know until later is that from the start, Leslie has done an extra workout each day, seven days a week, of 5 to 10 miles—this in addition to what the cross-country coach demands of all her runners.

The roommates admire Leslie's academic self-discipline but tease her quite a lot about the hours she puts in at her desk every night of the week—until they realize that she doesn't respond well to their teasing and is frantic if her effort doesn't produce A's on every problem set and quiz. Sometimes in response, she screams at them for not striving for perfection and, in a condescending way, tries to impose her standards on them. There is some hint in the way she talks about academic perfection of certain expectations on the part of her parents, but no one can quite put a finger on exactly what those expectations are. When her mother and father come for Parents Weekend in October, the roommates agree that they seem very nice and not very pushy.

The room is tense and uncomfortable, but nobody compares notes with anybody else or voices a suspicion about what might really be going on until after winter break, when everybody comes back to college after two weeks away. Leslie looks as though she has lost a lot of weight and might even have dipped below 100 pounds for the first time. Because she is a runner, everybody had thought she was just in good shape, but in January it is finally undeniable that she is anorexic—undeniable, that is, except by Leslie herself.

Leslie's RA confronts her with his concern and his suspicion that she has an eating disorder. She denies it, though she admits to having had such a problem briefly in high school. She refuses to go to the health service and tells him to leave her alone. He is asking questions about matters that are none of his business, she says, and he has no business invading her privacy this way.

The questions to be asked about Leslie's situation are different from those to be asked about Truman's. This isn't misconduct, nor is it substance abuse—exactly. Something is happening to her. She isn't sick in any of the usual ways. She isn't having trouble getting around (quite the contrary—she is a vigorous athlete); she isn't running a fever or complaining about headaches. Her academic performance isn't suffering. If you are one of Leslie's roommates, how, in the early stages, do you give a name to your feeling that she is in trouble? In her withdrawal, perfectionism, and loss of weight, she forces herself to the center of everybody's attention but also refuses to open up, so everybody is kept off balance. She is hurting herself, though it is hard to see exactly how at the beginning. She is not poisoning herself with huge quantities of alcohol or taking too many pills. Because the way she is behaving is not just subtly disturbing the people around her but is also potentially self-destructive, it is critical to admit to yourself that something is wrong, take her situation seriously, try to get her help, and confront her.

## ROMANCE

Julian meets Ann the third night of freshman week at a band concert on the steps of the chapel. From that moment on, they are inseparable. Julian is a shy fellow who hadn't dated much in high school. Ann is beautiful, intelligent, funny, and sophisticated. He is head over heels in love for the first time. They have meals together, go for coffee together every afternoon, study together, and soon are sleeping together in Ann's room. Ann has a roommate who seems very understanding. Julian and Ann do not even have to say very much to her. The roommate comes into the room a couple of times when they are there on the bed, talking or reading to each other, and soon has quietly moved all her things out of the bedroom and set up an area for herself in the living room.

Ann competes successfully for a place on the editorial board of the student-published journal on international affairs. Julian does nothing. He has no energy for anything or anyone but Ann. He can't study without her—only when they are together can he sit still with a book. He can't study with her, either, since he is so distracted by her and can think of nothing else when they are together. He runs errands for her, does their laundry while she is at the journal office, and drives her in his old car to her family's home on the weekends. His own parents spend some time with Julian and Ann and afterwards tell him they worry because he is spending so much time with her that he hardly seems to be at college. Julian will hear none of it.

Ann helps him through his first set of final exams. He barely passes, even with her considerable help. At midsemester, the dean asks Julian to come in for a chat about his academic performance and a concern voiced by Julian's roommates that they have seen almost nothing of him around the room since freshman week and have been worried that he is involved with drugs in a way he can't control. Julian is so paralyzed at the thought of talking with the dean that he asks Ann to go with him. She takes it on herself to meet with the dean ahead of time to reassure her that there are no drugs in Julian's life and that he is doing just fine—just having a hard time adjusting to college life and new love. The dean is not persuaded and wants to see Julian anyway.

Julian says almost nothing during the conference. Ann does all his talking for him. Very soon the dean has heard enough and sends them on their way.

Julian's situation, too, may be hard for a friend to figure out and certainly to think critically about. His roommates don't have it quite right when they take their worries to the dean. And have they done what they should have? No, he is not very involved in going to college; yes, he is wasting his parents' money. But this is his first experience with love, which is often confusing in just the ways he is experiencing. There is a hint that Ann is controlling him, but if that's so he'll figure it out soon enough. Anyway, it's his choice. They're not hurting anyone else. Julian should just be allowed to grow up at his own pace.

Think back over these stories, admittedly fragmentary and slanted accounts. Can we find ways to talk about them that are not preachy? What themes do they share? How are they different? Are there ways in which you can link the different stories to each other so that together they raise good questions for you about some of the disturbing things that happen to people in college?

## **HELP OR INTERFERENCE?**

Again, one of the questions that come up naturally is whether it is appropriate for a friend or a roommate, an adviser or a dean to look hard at the behavior or the relationships of a student so long as they remain private and do not encroach on public space. Especially in college, where the commitment to intellectual freedom and freedom of choice is supposed to be so strong, shouldn't students have a lot of leeway to make choices about how they want to live, even if the choices turn out to be mistakes?

The answer to this last question is a qualified "yes." But part of the difficulty of each of these stories is that the behavior hasn't remained private. Truman's frustration over lost athletic opportunity and his alcohol abuse (and possible alcoholism) lead, in very short order, to violence. Leslie's manipulation of her friends causes them to feel a pressing responsibility they never bargained for and that begins to keep them from paying attention to much else. Julian's obsession with Ann lets him collaborate with her, passively to be sure, in closing her roommate out of a bedroom the roommate has a right to and leads him to neglect his academic work. Sometimes we do walk a fine line trying to decide whether to intervene; we've said before that privacy is a value that needs to be protected vigorously in a college.

But violence is unacceptable. Manipulation of Leslie's sort is unfair. Neglect of work violates the compact a student makes with the college upon accepting admission. So in various ways, sometimes clearly, sometimes only arguably, it is appropriate to consider getting into the situation, depending on your relationship with the protagonist of the story. If you are a friend, you will ask one sort of question; if you were the dean, you might ask another. In either case, you'd be trying at some point to restore perspective. Hesitating to get involved is understandable, but helping and even asking someone else who has more experience to help are easy to distinguish from intruding or squealing—especially when your concern for someone else is about addiction or other general loss of control—about a pattern, not so much about a particular isolated incident.

## How Might You Help?

How you act will depend on the sort of relationship you have with the person involved. It's not hard to see each of these stories as stories about control and balance. In each situation, there is a promise that pain, of loneliness or disappointment, for example, will be taken away. The seductions promise security, allow no room for doubt or skepticism, and take away choice. Rena is even told by the Teacher that there is only one way to read the Book. In a college or university whose purpose is to encourage students to develop along lines that together describe a journey called a college education, it is essential to try to maintain enough control over your circumstances that you can exercise good critical judgment, make considered choices, and learn from the consequences of your actions. In each of these stories, important educational opportunities are severely limited.

You may not see much difference between some of these cases and the situation of a student who becomes so deeply involved in the college newspaper, theater productions, or a sport that he or she earns disappointing grades, or even the sort of grades that lead to an enforced vacation from college. However, there is an important difference: In the case of someone who becomes too committed to an extracurricular activity, the commitment is usually part of a conscious compromise, a choice to emphasize this rather than that, to learn in this way rather than that, to pursue excellence in this way rather than in that. When the commitment isn't part of a conscious compromise, however, it may not be very different from compulsion or other self-destructive behavior.

So you may have a hard time reading a real-life story very well as it is happening (you may need special help in reading if you are the main character) and then deciding what you want to do about it. If you become the main character in such a story, you can expect people who care about you to begin asking questions, at the very least, and those people will include teachers and deans, not just other students. If you are a neighbor or friend, you can expect encouragement from the college to take care of the other person. An educational community, like other communities, depends on people taking care of one another—even if that means saying things you're not sure you have a right to say.

*The first thing to do is to form the committees:
The consultative councils, the standing committees,
select committees and subcommittees.*

(T.S. Eliot)

# 14
# *Threading the Administrative Maze*

You probably won't have much reason in your first year to think about the administration of your college, especially if things go well, but you will be affected by administrative policies and procedures from the beginning of your college career. You will have to get yourself entered accurately into the college's records. You will face deadlines, and late fees if you miss them. You will enter into formal contracts with the college covering your room and your meals. You will take your final exams according to a schedule of specific times and places. The bureaucracy will require you to pay attention to its policies and procedures and occasionally to stand in line in an office or two. Though it will all seem a normal part of the familiar business of going to school, and though you had to do all this back in high school, only standing in shorter lines, bureaucracy will sometimes be wearying.

> *Things seem a lot better now than before, but it might just be the spring air. It takes a lot of adjustment to figure out this college's sprawling bureaucracy.*

## GOVERNMENT AND MANAGEMENT

There are at least three kinds of occasions on which you might have more pointed dealings with the college and begin to wonder about something you call The Administration. In all of these instances you might want to know who is in charge, how things are run, and why things are run this way.

- You might need an exception made to a rule. You might, for example, have dietary needs that the food service doesn't seem to be able to meet with its regular menus, so you ask to be excused from your meal contract. Or your sister is getting married in Hawaii on the day of your final in Physics 1, so you need to take the exam at a different place and time from those prescribed by the registrar.
- You might want to get something new accomplished. You might want to found a gallery to display artwork done by

students and need both a site and funding. Or you might want the people who run the computer center to substitute plain, perforated paper for the green-striped, unperforated paper they use in the terminal room.
- You might want to see some sweeping policy change at the college—changes in the investment policies of the board of trustees or the hiring practices of the dean of the faculty and the president.

These questions lead us to the broader issue of how a college is governed. This is worth understanding in a general way from the start, since how the college is governed determines in large measure how it is managed. Especially if you intend to become involved in student government or if from experience you expect to find yourself in active political opposition to the college, you will want to know where responsibility, authority, and power lie.

## The Trustees

If the college "belongs" to anyone, it is the trustees. They are entrusted by the charter, which establishes the college under state law, with choosing the president, granting degrees, seeing that the mission of the college is carried out, as well as with preserving the college's strength. Board members are supposed to ask hard questions about what the president, the faculty, and the students are doing. Trustees will ordinarily not be educators, whose theories might come into conflict inappropriately with the notions of the people running the college day to day, but men and women prominent in their professions—law, business, medicine, government—well connected and able to represent the interests of the college to the outside world. The questions the board members address to the president are supposed to reflect other perspectives, posed by people who understand how to run other sorts of complicated institutions. The board will meet three or four times a year, and most of its work will be done by small, powerful committees. Trustees will take the lead in long-range planning and in any major effort to raise funds for the college. A wise board will not interfere in the management of the college, but can fire the president and appoint a new one.

## The President

The president is accountable to the board. He or she must report to the board regularly on the college's progress in fulfilling its mission, on new programs, on the major issues being worked on by faculty and students, and on the financial condition of the college. To do this, and to be an effective leader and executive for the board, the president must know what is happening in every quarter and be in touch, directly or indirectly, with all constituencies, including alumni and other sources of financial support. So the president appoints vice presidents, the provost, and the deans to help in this task. The structure and number of these appointments will depend on the size and complexity of the college.

## The Senior Administration

These senior officers, some of whom may come from the faculty, serve as a kind of cabinet for the president and extend his or her executive authority into all the departments of the college. The vice presidents are responsible for such areas as finance, administration, legal counsel, government and community relations, fund-raising, and alumni affairs; the deans are responsible for the composition and structure of the faculty, the curriculum and academic rules, the quality of student life and discipline, and admissions and financial aid; and the provost functions as the president's general second in command. The deans will probably be appointed from the ranks of the faculty, while the vice presidents will not.

The deans and the vice presidents appoint assistant deans and directors. The areas of responsibility of these officers are many: facilities maintenance, the health service, dormitories and food service, personnel, security, athletics, the library, academic record keeping, financial operations, student services (counseling, advising, career services, residential life), annual alumni contributions—the list is often longer, even at a small college. The directors and assistant deans appoint and supervise staff with even more particular responsibility: sending out student term bills, operating the circulation desk at the library, coaching a sport, supervising custodial services in the dorms, organizing campus employment, running the shuttle bus, and so forth. They also hire and train the clerical staff for all the college offices.

## The Academic Departments

The dean of the faculty and the president persuade a member of the faculty in each department, program, and research center to take on the responsibilities of chairing that unit, usually for a specified term and sometimes in exchange for a slight reduction in teaching load. The chairman organizes the recruitment of new faculty by his or her department and the recommendations of the department for promotion and tenure. He or she ascertains that the courses offered by the department cover the field in as complete and balanced a way as possible. The chairman is responsible for the operating budget of the department and for keeping track of the efforts of the members to secure funding from sources outside the college to support their research. He or she also hires and supervises the department's clerical staff.

## Budgets and Planning

From a student's point of view, the matter of budgets may seem irrelevant and not very interesting, but it will often affect the college's response to requests from student groups for special funds or new programs. The income and expenses a department expects during the year are outlined in the budget. Expenses are always kept low, on orders from the dean or the vice president, in part because the college is trying hard to prevent tuition and room-and-board charges from increasing too fast. Control over expenditures will be quite centralized, too, even in some otherwise informal and apparently disorganized colleges, so getting a decision about even an apparently small expenditure is often difficult because so few people have the authority to spend money. Sometimes money isn't spent where a student sees an obvious need, and sometimes resources seem wasted.

> *Let me now address some of the bad stuff. Number one on my list is the condition of the freshman dorms. In short, they are pathetic. Not only was the place disgustingly filthy when I walked in in September, but the lighting is grossly insufficient, the bathrooms are rarely cleaned, and the place is falling apart everywhere. The heat was repeatedly turned off for no apparent reason; my RA would telephone the custodial service, and they wouldn't even make up an excuse but just admit that they had turned it off to save money. For the price we're paying to live here, I think they could leave the heat on. On a more trivial note, I don't think the custodian could be any more rude or unpleasant. Going to get toilet paper (during his few and far between hours of business) turned into an exercise in avoiding his wrath.*

> *I am more than a little annoyed at the gross amount of waste at this college. The libraries are ridiculously overheated—in the dead of winter a sweater is too warm. Even if fuel conservation weren't a factor, it's still true that being too hot makes people lethargic and unable to study well. In our dormitory, we lived through the entire year with our hinged window permanently open three inches to combat the fierce breath of our impassioned radiator, except for the times when the wind was blowing from the east. On those occasions, we had to hang a towel from the curtain to keep the draft from blowing our papers around. We have storm windows, but how about insulation? And on a smaller scale, what happens (I can guess) to the extra pans of pancakes/eggs/French toast that are whisked away at the stroke of 9:30 every morning? Surely it wouldn't be so very difficult to leave them out and let latecomers help themselves?*

## GOVERNANCE

Someone has to make the decisions about how the college will spend the money it has available for day-to-day operations, and so we are led to the question of how budgetary priorities are set. This question leads us away from descriptions of administration and management to questions of governance again.

The trustees delegate responsibility for short-range planning and financial matters to the president and his or her cabinet. The cabinet identifies the needs that can be met by centralized services. The whole faculty identifies the needs of the academic departments and programs or the necessary curricular reforms. In some colleges, the deans and vice presidents then establish the priorities of the college for the next year. (The provost may chair these sessions.) In some colleges, the discussion of priorities is broader; there is a collegewide committee, sometimes even called the priorities committee, in which faculty members, deans, and students hear presentations from officers with major budgetary responsibility, and then all participate in recommending priorities to the president.

### Student Government

Students participating in such discussions, even if the conferences occur in a fragmented and decentralized way, will probably be sent by student government. Student government might be based on geographical divisions. In such a case, each dormitory or cluster of dormitories might send a number of representatives to a central council. The officers are usually elected by the members of the council, not by students at large. The council does most of its important work, work respected by students and faculty alike, in committees that correspond roughly to the relevant standing committees of the faculty on which there are student members. So when student representatives sit with the faculty members on the joint committees, they bring the results of the deliberations of the corresponding student government committees.

The following are examples of topics that might come up in student government meetings.

- The proposal to impose a student activities fee or, if such a fee is already assessed, how grants will be made to student organizations that have applied for support.
- The future of fraternities and sororities, responding to a concern being expressed in the faculty following an incident of illegal hazing or some damage done in town by fraternity members.
- The status of ROTC—i.e., whether to urge the faculty to allow students enrolled in ROTC to receive course credit.
- The absence in the curriculum of courses dealing with non-Western cultures.
- The rules governing the use of alcohol on campus.
- Freedom of speech, responding both to a student demonstration at the speech of a controversial figure the previous spring and to the anger of minority students over remarks made in a professor's lecture that were construed as insulting to Asian Americans.

## How Are Decisions Made?

Sometimes student government's actions or decisions will be binding on students; sometimes student government will recommend action to the faculty or the deanery that will affect students. Student government's authority will often depend on how much power the faculty has delegated to it. The faculty's authority comes from the board of trustees. The faculty will certainly have authority in all matters relating to the curriculum and granting degrees and probably will also be responsible for disciplinary actions.

Administrative members of the joint committees will sometimes propose ideas for discussion and submit proposals for legislation by the faculty and student government. They will often take direction from the committees when proposed work falls within areas of administrative discretion and responsibility. Sometimes the deliberations of a committee will have the status of advice for a dean—legislation will not be appropriate. It may be within the jurisdiction of the dean to decide whether to follow the committee's recommendations.

But very often the status of a recommendation from a governing body or a committee to a dean will not be so clear because the constitution and bylaws are not detailed enough or the traditions of the college don't speak clearly enough. Then the course of events will depend on goodwill and a tolerance for seemingly endless consultation. Sometimes goodwill and tolerance won't be enough, and the result will be mistrust and acrimony that will embitter discussions in the college for months. Usually, careful and patient consultation with all involved parties will move the situation along to a new and reasonably stable place.

The rules that apply to the issue raised—whether it is how to get a late-fee waived, how to get financial support for a project, or how to get a new category of courses introduced into the curriculum—may be a product of faculty legislation, student government legislation, or administrative policies and procedures consistent with the intentions of the faculty. Rule making in a college is slow business. An apparently straightforward proposition may take as long as two years, half your stay in college, to achieve the status of rule. Change comes slowly, in part because committees must be formed and everybody must consult. But in addition, part of a college's mission is to preserve and transmit knowledge, what the best minds have argued about the way the world works; so changes in the curriculum or in the degree requirements will come slowly, as members of the faculty try to ensure that part of their mission is not jeopardized. The board of trustees bears much responsibility for the future of the college, so members will insist that nothing be done that will jeopardize the future. It shouldn't be surprising, therefore, that when you approach an office with what seems to you a relatively simple matter, the response will sometimes seem conservative. Conserving is part of what colleges must do. This can sometimes lead to the attitude that what is, is right.

*My only comment to the administration as a whole would be to be careful about being pretentious.*

## EFFECTING CHANGES

Then how does anything exceptional ever get done? How do any bold moves ever get made? You will have to work your way through the maze of administrative authority until you reach the right office and the right desk and talk to the right person, who can help you do what you want to do. You may well need help in the first place figuring out how to do this. Your adviser is a good person to start with—even if he or she doesn't think that what you want to do is such a good idea.

Once you have your route through the maze mapped out, you need to commit yourself to your goal and frame the best arguments you can in support of your idea, taking into account the most forceful counterarguments you might meet. So you will need to figure out why the present situation is as it is, put yourself in the shoes of the administrator responsible, and try to guess what risks your request or petition represents to that person. Getting an accurate reading on the recent history of the issue will not be easy; neither will figuring out which office combines just the right mix of authority and responsibility. But if you want to get anywhere, you will need to do good political spadework, whether you are petitioning individually to be released from your meal contract because you have an ulcer, or you are part of a group from student government trying to develop a plan for storing students' furniture and other belongings over the summer. In the first instance, keeping students on contract may be so important to the budget that the director of food services is willing to design special menus for people with special medical needs, and the dean has decided that such an effort must be made before he or she will consider releasing a student. In the second case, the director of residences may have been too frantically busy for years to think about summer storage, or he or she has thought about it but so far hasn't come up with a plan that provides adequate security.

Not every situation will be so difficult. Sometimes what you want to accomplish will be easily done, so you will be pleasantly surprised and won't worry about negotiating until the next time you need something. Sometimes you will not be able to accomplish what you need to, and it will only be a matter of having come up against overworked and underpaid people in a college office who, in their exhaustion and frustration, can't or won't see a way to help you. And then you'll have to decide how important the matter is to you and what you want to do about being stymied. As you consider next steps, you may find yourself poised between treating the person behind the desk as a human being or as some disembodied hindrance to the pursuit of your goal. Sometimes exchanges will reach the frayed edges of someone's patience—yours or, as in the following case, the other person's.

> *This is based on hearsay and I hope it's not true, but I will pass it on. A friend who was trying out for the newspaper called up the dean at one point for a comment and apparently was rather rudely snubbed. Now, I understand that he may have interrupted dinner, that the dean's mother-in-law may have been over, or whatever, but my friend's motives were quite innocent and rudeness is never justified. Some people at the newspaper may not stir deans with warmth and good feeling, but there are a lot of us who like the school, are favorably disposed to the administration, and sincerely want comment. So please . . . give the reporter the benefit of the doubt.*

## **WHAT ARE DEANS FOR, ANYWAY?**

In many colleges, the administrative officer who is in the best position to help a student or a group of students to be heard is a dean. A dean also is often in a position to discourage students' efforts to have an exception made or to accomplish a reform. It is doubly useful, then, to understand what a dean does, especially since, even if your high school had a dean or two, the job description was probably different. Let's locate this dean in imaginary administrative space somewhere between the president and the registrar. You can tell from the student handbook and from dealings you and other students have with the office that the registrar's job is to enforce all the rules that govern how students qualify for their degrees—the rules of enrollment, submission of work, conduct of examinations, and academic progress. The president's job is not so easy to understand. He is rarely seen except on state occasions or when there is a campus crisis. You know that the president has important dealings with the board and with the senior officers in the administration. Despite having a reputation for always accepting any invitation from a student or a group of students, he seems remote.

The dean appears to have more general and immediate responsibility for the welfare of students. Unlike the sadistic figure in *Animal House*, he does not appear to have it in for students. Consider this scenario, which isn't so farfetched. In early October, you and other freshmen on your floor get an invitation to tea at the dean's house. As you talk, you ask what deans are for, anyway. Taking your question seriously, he asks you to visit the office for an answer. It turns out that he is in charge of academic and general advising in the freshman year, oversees the work of the orientation committee, ensures that the dormitories are safe and sound and that people can learn there from one another, advises student organizations, acts as academic adviser to a dozen freshmen, teaches a course in contemporary philosophy, serves on the discipline committee and the committee on examinations and standing (where exceptions to the registrar's rules are made), and in general keeps his door open to any student who has a question that hasn't yet been answered, who has an idea but doesn't know where to take it next, or who is in pain. Sometimes the door leads into his home.

> *I came to your tea and was grateful not only to have had the chance to be in a real house with a real dog, a real kid, and real, edible food, but also to have met you both. Several weeks later, I am still grateful. It struck me as I read that unsent thank-you note that the tea is the sort of thing that makes college civilized. To feel welcome in your house, not just as another tuition-paying student, one of thousands to pass through over the course of years, but as a person with a reason for being here, was really nice. It is the warmth and humor of the "curators" of my education here that inspire me.*

The dean who explains his work to you happens to be dean of freshmen, but he might be the dean of students or the dean of the college and give a similar account of a dean's work. Whether making budgets, supervising staff, or overseeing the operation of programs, a dean's work is keeping the college open and flexible and its resources useful to students and faculty. On many days the work will take the mundane shape of trying to make sure people are talking clearly with the appropriate other people in order to accomplish worthy educational purposes. In the case of the dean you talk with at tea, this may even mean making sure students feel confident about taking up certain questions with instructors—about their expectations in a course, the possibility of getting an extension on a lab assignment, or the meaning or importance of a midyear exam grade.

## STUDENT OPINION

How are students' voices, other than those of the student government, heard? What does student opinion count for in the operation or reform of the college? The answers to these questions are not simple. There is no standard procedure. You should prepare yourself to feel, at least some of the time, that you have not been heard; you probably will have been heard, in fact, but you may feel otherwise. You say to the committee on examinations and standing that you did write the paper your instructor claims never to have received in the mail. Couldn't you just have an extension to rewrite it, because unfortunately you didn't make a copy in the first place? The response will probably be no, because the committee will be concerned about fairness to the other students in the class, but you will feel that they should take circumstances beyond your control into account. Their concern for equity will seem irrelevant to your case. Or a group of students will feel that its race or ethnic group has been insulted by an article in the parody issue of the newspaper and demand that the dean shut the paper down. The dean may refuse and suggest in turn that there be a collegewide discussion of free speech, journalistic ethics, and artistic license. You may feel as though the dean has missed the point. Or you will read in the paper that the president has taken a position that puts him in the opposite camp from the majority of students on an issue of shareholder responsibility, and you join the general murmur of "unresponsive administration." Yet in this case, the board of trustees may have weighed the opinions of students very carefully and still have decided that their responsibility for the future of the college demands that they support the president's position. In these circumstances, you may have to guard against cynicism.

> *The administration? More concerned with PR than anything else.*

On the other hand, the deanery may decide that it makes all the sense in the world to reform the room assignment process for sophomores in the way students have suggested. Or the faculty may agree with students that a required ethnic studies course should be established. In those cases, you and other students are likely to feel, naturally, that the faculty and the administration are very responsive.

In the best case, the committee or the individual who has the responsibility to make a decision will listen to the opinions of all the constituencies that will be affected by the decision. But when the decision is made, it is unlikely that everybody will be satisfied. So in the best case there will be a careful explanation of the considerations involved in the ruling when the decision is announced, and everyone in the college will feel fairly heard. Sometimes, though, the considerations can't be stated publicly, or the critical nature of the situation will demand that a decision be made before the need for full consultation has been satisfied. Sometimes an individual personality, a clash of personalities, or some political tactic will force things to happen too fast or move in an unfortunate direction. This will occasionally just happen, even when people's intentions are good, and there won't be much anybody can do about it. In some such cases, a request for reconsideration that is well argued and strongly supported will be successful, and the discussion can get back on track.

Remember that most of these administrative issues will be

deep in the background of your experience in the first year or two of school. Occasionally, though, you will touch the college's political nervous system, so it's important to have some understanding of how things work. Only then will you be able to come to a sensible judgment about whether things are fair in a case you care about. Most of the time it will all seem to work reasonably well.

> *The bureaucracy was accessible and helpful to a certain extent, but most guidance came from other students.*
>
> *In fact the bureaucracy did help me somewhat just by being composed of a friendly bunch of individuals. . . . They were always helpful, easygoing, and friendly. They provided information about areas of interest to me. . . . The individuals involved in the bureaucracy provided information that, taken all together, leads me to both new and existing interests. To that extent, they made the transition to college life easier.*
>
> *I appreciated the laissez-faire attitude of the administration; nonetheless, its weekly newsletter reminded me that there was someone out there to help, just in case.*

*We are plain quiet folk and have no use for adventures. Nasty disturbing uncomfortable things! Make you late for dinner! I can't think what anybody sees in them.*
                                (Bilbo Baggins)

*It is a liberty to choose how one will relate to, contribute to, and cooperate with one's fellow men, a liberty to define, develop and control what will give one satisfaction, a liberty to develop some and not other capacities, in short, the liberty to determine a life plan, to choose one's self.*
                                (Charles Fried)

*For a whale ship was my Yale College and my Harvard.*
                                (Melville)

# 15
# *Shaping Your Own Education*

This last chapter suggests ways of seeing your education as a whole, rather than as unconnected rules, requirements, courses, extracurricular choices, and roommate crises.

College students begin to find a direction by struggling to make sense of decisions they knew they would face but that seem impossible, now that they are actually facing them, in their number and intensity. Almost nobody walks from high school into college with a fully developed philosophy of education. So take the questions you've already got about college—what it will be like and how you'll manage—and the questions in the introductory chapter of this book—what's important to you, what you're good at, what you like, what you want—and think about beginning to frame an argument based on those questions. It will be an argument you carry on first with yourself and then with others—friends, parents, advisers, and teachers—once you're ready.

## **BEGINNING**

As a first step, imagine yourself home for the summer after your freshman year. You are enthusiastically describing to your friends the courses you have taken and what you are thinking about studying. You tell your friends about your courses in composition, ethics, elementary physics, and Portuguese, and hear from them about their courses in pharmacology, legal writing, accounting, and systems design. They are premed, prelaw, and prebusiness, and when they ask what you are getting ready to do with your life, you have no quick and easy answer. Your friends know where they are going. You are reading difficult books in a course called Moral Reasoning and trying out a language you know you will never use. It is going to take character to stick with this conversation and not propose a trip to the lake. But in the relative leisure of summer, you begin to think again about the meaning and shape of your education, to hear echoes of high school graduation speeches, to look again at what you said on your admission applications, to think about what you dismissed as platitudes in the president's speech at convocation in September.

College may not seem to prepare you for any particular next step. You may be trying on the idea of education for its own sake. Defending that, even to yourself, can sometimes be a hard job. If you approach the tasks of college as though they have to be preparation for a particular career or for graduate study in a profession—thinking, for example, that you have to study political science or biology or economics in order to get on in the world—you may find yourself entangled in contradictions and frustrations that can damage your enthusiasm and, just as important, cause you to miss opportunities that will later be a source of regret.

## PUTTING TOGETHER AN ARGUMENT

Without some effort of imagination, your education might remain only a collection of fragments, because few college experiences can be explained in light of obvious careers. How to go about making this effort? Beginning in the spring and summer before you leave for college and working at it for as long as necessary (which may turn out to be many years), assemble an argument for your education—keeping a journal, writing letters to friends, even taking long, quiet walks. Don't do this to protect yourself against questions from your friends and the expectations of your parents and teachers, but to make sense for yourself of what you are doing. It can be an argument you improvise and continually revise. No one else can tell you how it should go, though you will find plenty of material in the advice of others. Framing this argument may not be the same as stating particular, concrete goals. It may be about what you like and how you want to grow.

One such argument might begin this way: Math and science come easily to me, but the most exciting thing I did in high school was to write a five-page paper on *The Merchant of Venice*. As I understand it, college is supposed to give me a chance to figure out why I liked doing that paper so much, so I'm going to keep going in math and English until I know which area is more satisfying. Just as important is my singing. I need to know whether I'm really any good at that.

Or, this way: Math is immensely satisfying. My teachers have told me that I have real potential. I'd rather read a math text on problems I haven't had in class than a murder mystery. As I understand it, college will let me work in real depth in the field of my choice, so I'm going to pursue math as far as I can. My college will probably insist that I study other subjects as well, but I think I will learn as much about the way people have thought about the world by doing math as other students will by exploring other fields.

Or: I have no idea what I want to do with my time in college. I believe that a college education will get me ready to think intelligently when I am out in the world. Maybe it doesn't matter what I major in so long as I'm doing something that interests and challenges me. I like thinking about the way people interact; maybe for a while I'll pick friends and courses and activities that let me understand as much as I can about what it means to be a social animal.

In each case the argument is based on a view of the value of education. It takes into account both what others have said about your strengths and weaknesses and what you know about what satisfies you, and it begins to organize your choices. The argument isn't grandiose, it's practical; and most important it's a beginning. It doesn't lock you in. It's a guide for decisions; it's flexible and open to revision. It is a framework, an attempt to map the journey before you set out, a way of starting that makes sense to you. This student is beginning to lay out just such an argument.

> *I guess that's what coming to college is all about—learning to learn for yourself and not judge things at face value. It's also coming in contact with things that have never affected you before—like the homeless problem.*

## Other Approaches

There are other ways of framing the argument that are fun—whimsical even. In your sophomore year in high school, your

Latin teacher recognizes that you are a strong student who ought to go to an excellent college. He invites you to drive with him and his daughter, who is something of a soccer star and a computer whiz, to a reception held by alumni of his college to give potential applicants an opportunity to hear from a member of the college's admission staff. You worry that all the talk will be about soccer, but people talk to you, not just to the soccer star. On the way back, your teacher treats you to a lecture on the medieval idea of the liberal arts. There were seven arts, he says, organized into a group of four—arithmetic, geometry, astronomy, and music—called the quadrivium, and a group of three—grammar, rhetoric, and logic—called the trivium. Hence the word "trivial," he says, beaming pedantically. You fall asleep, but the little lecture stays with you, and later, when you are casting about for a way to organize your approach to your own education, you decide (why not?) to begin by using the model of the quadrivium and the trivium. If it was good enough for scholars in the Middle Ages it's good enough for you—at least as a way to get started, helping you choose your first math course or decide whether to participate in debate.

Or you have decided to attend a college that was founded in the early nineteenth century to train young men for the ministry. The college has shed much of its religious tradition by now, and you come to it from a different tradition, anyway, but you decide in a sort of bet with yourself to see whether you can find a way through the curriculum that imitates what you imagine the early training of preachers to have been. "If I imagine myself studying to become a preacher," you say to yourself, "how would I go about it in a secular way?" So you decide you must take courses in the origins of the universe, ancient and modern history, folklore, comparative religion, and public speaking—at least that's your plan at the start.

Or you could argue from a perspective of sheer improvisation, as though your approach to your education were going to be like the moves of a jazz piano player. You will try at each stage of your way through college to understand how what you are doing now gives shape to what you will do next and shows you ways of getting there. You won't have a four-year plan, at least at the beginning, but you will pay attention to what your hands are doing on the keyboard of the college, so to speak, so that you begin to feel where they must go next.

You may be more comfortable with less whimsy and find the elements of an argument for your education in a book on the subject—in Plato's *Republic, The Education of Henry Adams,* C. P. Snow's *The Two Cultures,* or the autobiographical writing of Einstein, W. E. B. DuBois, Eudora Welty, or Lewis Thomas. In fact, searching out the elements of an argument might determine how and what you read during the summer before you leave for college.

Whether or not any of these ways of putting together the rudiments of an argument for your education seem just right, in each case the method is chosen freely and provides a place to start, not a place to finish. Saying that you want to be a lawyer and must complete a prelaw curriculum, and saying this before you have any idea what attorneys do or because you think you have to choose a career since everybody else has, might keep you from discovering the range of experiences available to you in college. You need room to maneuver, explore, improvise, and make fundamental changes in your plans if you are ever to find a satisfying way of college life and work.

A sense of where you're going probably won't come to you out of the blue or from a change of personality.

> *You didn't, unfortunately, give me the sense of direction I longed for. I filled out my plan of study (including choosing a department almost at random) the afternoon of the day it was due. I'll have to think a lot over the summer.*

> *Overall, this year did not cause any overwhelming change in my life, habits, or thoughts. I still have very little idea of the future (by this I mean I have no ambition for working toward a set, concrete goal 10 years from now—i.e., a career). I don't think my character has undergone any fundamental change. But then again, this is only my first year at college. No doubt (or at least I hope so) by the end of my stay here, I will have at least some direction for my future.*

## EDUCATION AS PREPARATION

Looked at as a way to the future, a college education may not be preparation for anything in particular, but it is certainly a particular sort of preparation. Spend some time talking with people who have been through college and discover what they did and what they think about it now, looking back. You might well hear about missed opportunity. They may say they regret not exploring more widely, not taking their time with their undergraduate education, rushing to get on with their professions and their careers. They may tell you they should have taken more of those seemingly irrelevant courses that looked so tempting: philosophy, art history, music appreciation, the introductory math and science courses they were scared of, more of the foreign language they thought then that they would never need. The message seems to be that the value of college is something other than just getting through it, that life after college is more than just a job, and that the years go by faster than one sometimes realizes.

Listen to them. They are saying something important: You will see college differently in retrospect. One thing among many to think about, therefore, is how to be sure that the backward view is satisfying—that as an undergraduate you did what you wanted to do. This is hard to do since you haven't been through college yet—to envisage yourself looking back on your college experience from, say, 20 years out, and guessing what will be pleasing to you then, in memory.

You need not, and probably should not, construct a rigid system of priorities. Try to keep what is important to you in your sights all the time and be ready to play with new possibilities. Let your feelings about what interests you, operating in the light of what is important to you, govern what courses you take, what field or fields you concentrate in, what extracurricular activities you commit yourself to, and how deeply you commit yourself. Such an approach will allow you to make the largest number of good connections among the things you do. This is a plea against doing things in college automatically and a plea for recognizing and crediting your own integrity. Picture yourself doing things that interest you and then let your education be an expanding of the self you imagine.

## Choices

Though college may not provide preparation for particular kinds of work, it certainly can be preparation for citizenship, and even leadership. Control of your own life and productive membership in institutions always involve making significant choices—not just when you vote but even when you simply discuss important issues. You might think of your education as practice in making such choices, developing intellectual skills and habits that you can use effectively later, in whatever involvement in public life you undertake. Your undergraduate years can teach you to choose well and to defend your choices to others. Choices are real and important events. They take up time, and their consequences take up room in people's lives. They are not switches thrown semiautomatically. Choices can be thought about silently or out loud, their consequences can be anticipated and even weighed in advance, and over time they can embody your consistency and integrity. Your choices will speak for you.

## What You Will Learn

If you are lucky and work hard, you will learn to read and write in college. It may even be that this is the most one can hope to do, but it is surely a glorious hope. This doesn't mean only that you will graduate able to read with insight and judgment and write with the clipped and pointed grace valued by all people of "mature taste." Although these are worthy goals, given the resources that college will offer, you may go further and, through reading and writing, discover a different world or change yourself in ways that make a world of difference. Even so, you cannot hope to graduate from college an expert, though some people come very close. You will probably know a little bit about something, but you will certainly know almost nothing about anything else. You will even admit to it.

> *I've learned two things this year. One is that I could spend the rest of my life learning and barely scratch the surface. The other is that I can easily work every day, all day, for a whole semester, and not get everything done. But at least I learn a lot.*

So you might decide that you will read every book you can get your hands on that is rumored to be great, that you will refuse to accept everything you read, and that you will write your fingers to the bone. If you do these things, you will develop critical judgment, which will allow you to argue persuasively and honestly and will also allow you to admit that you have been persuaded. And, of course, the reading and writing you do need not be what English majors do, but could be what historians, political scientists, biologists, geologists, or physicists do. The tools and the topics of your reading and writing may be numbers.

This education, pursued with enthusiasm and energy, will affect your intellectual and personal development profoundly. Your basic skills will improve with constant exercise. You will read faster and with greater comprehension because it is demanded of you by your instructors and by the books. Because you will do laboratory experiments and write papers that require you to do research, you will learn something about gathering and using evidence. You will learn the basic steps of building a careful argument, in part because your freshman English instructor will ask you to develop thesis statements and draw conclusions that frame what comes between. When a course asks you to confront a Picasso drawing or a Louise Nevelson sculpture, or when an instructor asks you to break down a speech or an essay into its components so you can lay bare its logic, you will learn analysis. Assembling a view of the wrongheadedness of an op-ed piece on oil depletion allowances, you will practice responsible synthesis.

You will learn history, whether you take courses in the History Department or not. Each time you hear a voice from the past and answer it in your own voice or see resemblances between events of the past and what is happening now, you will be doing the work historians do. The same week you reread the

Gettysburg Address in your American lit survey, you may see an article in the magazine section of the Sunday paper on the Vietnam War memorial in Washington, and you will understand something about the way deaths of young people in battle can change how survivors understand national purpose. Don't resist learning history because you didn't enjoy it in high school. Someday you'll have to know what to do with precedents.

You will interpret symbols. At first you may simply stand before a symbol, not knowing what to do or if anything in particular is called for. Then you will begin to respond. This will happen on 100 different occasions in college, and you may not even recognize what is going on. You will be trying to solve an equation in multivariable calculus or describing a reaction in chemistry. You will be reading about how witch doctors in West Africa do psychotherapy. You will be trying to identify the objects in a thirteenth-century painting of St. Jerome or to make sense of a twentieth-century poem about a person called the Emperor of Ice Cream or a place called the Waste Land. Or you will find yourself writing a poem of your own and not being able to say what you feel about the importance of silence without embodying it in an object or a situation. In these situations you will begin to understand what makes something a symbol and when interpretation is appropriate.

You will practice criticism. This does not mean being negatively judgmental, but understanding something by analyzing it. In a film course, you will be struck by a resemblance between *Love Story* and *Dark Victory*. To make the idea clear in your paper, you will disassemble it into as many of its components as you can see. You will define terms carefully. You will avoid giving your reader summaries of the plots of the two movies (however many more pages that would allow you to write). You will try to make clear what the components of the idea, taken all together, let you say about the movies that you couldn't have said if you hadn't taken them apart. This account will be your synthesis, healing the "damage" done to the films by your analysis.

From time to time you will set out on quests. You will define a goal as fully as is required by your circumstances, lay out a plan of attack or an itinerary, and devote all your energies to achieving your goal. Not every endeavor in college will take this shape, but some ought to. Writing a thesis in your senior year or trying to be the best journalist or the best javelin thrower you can be are examples of quests. Such efforts will let you practice defining excellence and pursuing it.

## FINDING YOURSELF, GROUNDING YOURSELF

The intellectual work demanded by your courses will sometimes draw you toward a position on an issue or a way of seeing something—an event in a laboratory or a lyric poem—that you can distinguish from other perspectives. You will begin to recognize what positions you take because they are more or less comfortable and what positions you have to strain to take, and therefore realize what you believe and what you care about. It is as if, as you clarify your points of view in a world where you are frequently invited to argue by teachers and friends, your own outline and edges and limits become clearer. The intellectual process forces you to choose between values. Your sense of who and what you are is enhanced in the natural course of doing the work.

You will find what is right for you.

> *I think that if I had to characterize my freshman year, it would be as a time when I kept on trying things because felt I should and ended up, after a lot of pain, abandoning those things I didn't want to do. I kept trying to prove things to myself—I can survive as a math major, I can outargue the valedictorian next door, I can join lots of clubs, I can hold down a job and take five courses—and kept realizing that I shouldn't have to keep proving things to myself. As the year draws to a close, I'm surprised and quite satisfied at the me that's emerged. I'm much more independent than I guessed I would be. I don't feel nearly as much as I did that I need the acceptance of other people—my own self-approval is good enough most of the time. That's a kind of confidence I could have used earlier, and I'm glad I have it now. I no longer feel that others who*

> have talents are a threat to my talents (except during
> reading period, when I don't have time for self-confidence).
> I say that especially with reference to the two roommates I'll
> continue to live with next year. For the most part, I can
> cheer their successes and lament their failures without
> feeling they reflect on me, as I did at the beginning of the
> year. And that's the most wonderful thing that's come out of
> the year.

## Discernment

These personal developments will have implications for your political life. You won't necessarily label yourself radical, liberal, or conservative. You won't automatically become a more skillful leader or a shrewder follower, although you might. But in the course of sharpening your points of view and clarifying what you value, you will be able to recognize responsible and irresponsible uses of power in all sorts of contexts—first in relationships with roommates and friends and then in academic and bureaucratic settings. You will understand when people are manipulating others and when they are being unfair or hurtful. You will know why you admire fairness or ethical sensitivity.

You will also gain the confidence to challenge the positions of others when, in your judgment, they deserve to be challenged. Rather than letting some outrageous nonsense go by because nobody could possibly have meant what you just heard, you will wade in and take the risk of overstepping in order to set something right. You will also recognize signs of intellectual or moral arrogance in yourself.

These sorts of intellectual and social risk taking, experimentation, and personal development are possible because of freedom granted to students by the college and, sometimes grudgingly, by the larger society. You will be able to try on different attitudes and intellectual and political personas because the college believes it is important for you to have such leeway. But it isn't an inalienable right. If you begin to believe that, you are fooling yourself. Always remember that, at some point, you must go out into the world.

You are reading a book. The book isn't necessarily *Bleak*

*House* or an account of the economic interests of the Founding Fathers; it can be a cluster of physics problems or (figuratively) the college library. You are enthralled by what you are reading. The book is so difficult that you have to work on its parts before you can get the whole. You weigh the ideas you can make sense of in the scales of your imagination and judgment. In the process you find yourself in a conversation with the author, in which you question the premises on which the author stands. Your confidence, real and justified, sets you free to continue both to argue with the author and to hold on to your own convictions. The freedom you earn by hard intellectual work allows you also to be generous. You can be both open-minded and open-handed with what you learn. You may even feel that such generosity is required to complete the process of learning, that you will not really have learned until you have shared the material with someone else and offered up your ideas for testing. This teaching will be one of the ways you enrich the college community and one of the ways you will contribute to the communities you join later on.

## LIBER—LIBRA—LIBERTAS—LIBERALITAS

Reading a difficult book seriously leads to an openness of spirit. There is a pun in Latin in this section's heading that gives a way of asserting and even arguing, in shorthand, the ethical nature of college study. Once you see that ideas cannot remain the exclusive property of any one person for long, you may find reason to rethink the balance between competition and cooperation you want to characterize your approach to college life and work.

> *My personal goal is to be a human element of this college. I don't think the pursuit of grades should control the person, and I will never sequester myself behind a book when I know another person needs my help in any way. High school in no way prepared me for the zoo of competition I found here. But my standards haven't changed. I still prefer the freshman who dribbles a basketball through the*

> *dining hall during dinner to the freshman who knows all the implications of the Treaty of Versailles inside out but doesn't know when to laugh at a joke.*

Don't feel that you must take someone else's word on this. Work it out for yourself if you need to. But don't be surprised if college seems to you, at least for the first few weeks and months, an endless series of decisions to be made. In order not to be overwhelmed and exhausted by the rush of these new, demanding situations, you may need an anchor or two and a framework within which to arrange things. If you can imagine what college will be like, imagining it may make it a fuller and happier experience. If you can make pictures in your head of what it might be like for you once you enter college, some things will seem almost familiar when you get there, you will almost understand why some things are the way they are, and you will almost know what you will demand of yourself there, helped in all this by a hint of déjà vu.

## PUTTING OFF COLLEGE

Now that you think about it, moving toward and through college without wandering may not be the best direction for you.

> *To deviate from the ideal view, I'll mention something about getting away from college. Believe it or not, getting away is very important, even if only for a night on the town or to go back home during vacation. You can get a new perspective on what you're doing, where you're going, and what college is all about. I guess that's why so many people choose to take time off. Believe me, I've been away in the "real world" a lot. Each time I'm away from college, I appreciate and understand its workings more.*

You might even conclude that the time isn't ripe for you to be in college. It's one of the responses this book invites. You feel burned out or in need of seasoning. If you feel it would be better for you to take time off from school and to work or travel around the world rather than going to college right away, that may be exactly what you should do. It will take courage and work to reach such a conclusion legitimately and even greater courage and harder work to act well on it. People who love you may oppose the idea. You will need to present it carefully and patiently, taking their reasons into account together with your own. Too many people are in college without being ready or are there for reasons that are not their own. They are unhappy. Not being able to make their own kind of sense of what they are doing, they cannot get courses or requirements or extracurricular activities to make sense either. The educational process can't survive that sort of confusion for long. It demands clear-mindedness and enthusiasm.

College is not the only way to educate yourself. Taking a year off to earn your own money at a job at the local video store, to put yourself through a wilderness survival course in the Wind River Range, or to get yourself and a good friend by plane, train, and thumb to Greece and Yugoslavia may be just what you need to recover your enthusiasm for learning because you come to know, in ways that have nothing to do with school, the joys of exploration and the satisfactions of independence.

# INDEX

Absences, 48, 92–93
Academic departments, 121–122, 203
Achievement
  other peoples' views of, 29–30
  personal definition of, 28–29
Adjustment, to college, 22–23
Administration, college, 50, 56, 200–213
  academic departments, 121–122, 203
  budgets and planning, 203–204
  deans, 209–211
  making changes and, 208–209
  president, 202
  senior administration, 202–203
  student government, 205–207
  student opinion and, 211–213
  trustees, 201–202
Admissions committee, 31–32, 171–172
Advisers, 64, 102–103, 108–111
  advice on study skills from, 113–114
  in college major, 143–146
  course selection and, 108
  difficulties with, 109–111
  discussing assignments with, 108–109
  exams and, 109
  expectations concerning, 111–113
  informal advice and, 114–115
  planning and, 108, 109
  selection of a major and, 139–141
  *See also* Faculty
Advising center, 104
Affirmative action programs, 171–172
Agreements, written, 40, 42
Alcohol use, 105, 166–167, 173–174, 186–189, 191–192
Analysis, self-, 2–5
Anorexia nervosa, 193–194
Arguments, for a college education, 217–229
  developing, 217–220
  education as preparation, 221–225
  finding yourself, 225–227
  putting off college and, 228–229
Arts activities, 151–152
Assimilation, 182

Basic requirements, 66–67
Books, library, 50–53
Budgets and planning, 203–204
Bureaucracy. *See* Administration, college
Business activities, 153

Careers
  college major and choice of, 137–142, 147–148
  of faculty members, 120–121
  planning for, 105–106
Catalog, course. *See* Courses, catalog of
Categorical thinking, 181–184
Chairman, department, 203
Chaplains, 106, 113
Clichés, 173–174
Collaboration, 54–55, 78
College administration. *See* Administration, college
Commitment, extracurricular activities and, 158–159, 162–164
Comprehensive exams, 145
Compulsive behavior, 193–194
Conference courses, 71–72
Confidentiality, 113
Confusion, 17–23
  finances and, 20–21
  gains and losses and, 21–23
  parents' expectations and, 17–19
  teachers' expectations and, 17–19
  those left behind and, 19
Counseling center, 104–105
Counselors, 102–105
  peer, 107
Courses
  catalog of, 64–65, 67, 136–137
  exams and, 74–75, 109, 121, 145
  grades for, 72–74, 93, 110
  kinds of, 68–72
  literature, 90–99
  mathematics, 84–87
  prerequisite, 55
  reading for, 3, 83–84, 90–99, 222–227

science, 85–87
selecting, 64–67, 108
time management and, 31, 79–80, 113–114, 158–160
writing for, 3, 81–83, 90–99, 222–225
*See* Curriculum
Crisis counselors, 107
Criticism, 224
Cults, 188–191
Curiosity, 83
Curriculum
 basic requirements in, 66–67
 choosing courses, 64–65, 108
 design of, 65–66
 exams and, 74–75, 109, 121, 145
 grades and, 72–74, 93, 110
 kinds of classes, 68–72
 rules concerning, 50, 51, 55–56
 testing of rules and, 55–56
 *See also* Courses

Dating, 173–174, 194–195
Deadlines, 56, 78–79, 93
Deans, 209–211
Delaying college, 228–229
Departments, academic, 121–122, 203
Depression, 22, 105
Differences, 170–184
 assumptions and, 177–178
 awareness of personal, 5–7, 170–171
 categorical thinking and, 181–184
 clichés and, 173–174
 community support and, 181–184
 empathy and, 178–180
 generalizing about, 171–172
 identity and, 175–176
 learning from, 179–181
 prejudice of others and, 175
 respect and, 174–175
 responsibility and, 174
 self-image and, 177
 sexual orientation and, 172, 176–177, 183
 stereotypes and, 172–173
Discernment, 226–227
Discipline, 60–62, 113, 187–188
Discipline committee, 60–62
Dissertation, 126
Dormitory life, 36–46
 community and, 43–46
 dorm room, 36–37

 independence and, 37–38
 parties and, 165–167, 186–189
 roommates in, 38–46
Drug use, 105, 186–189

Eating disorders, 105, 193–194
Empathy, 178–180
Entitlement, myth of, 15–16
Evaluation. *See* Exams; Grades
Exams, 74–75, 121
 adviser and, 109
 general or comprehensive, 145
 grades and, 72–74
 studying for, 75
Expectations
 of high school teachers, 17–19
 of parents, 17–19
Extensions, 56, 78–79, 93
Extracurricular activities, 30–31, 150–167
 benefits of, 160–164
 parties and, 165–167, 186–189
 selecting, 150–160
 traditions and, 164–165
 types of, 151–154

Faculty, 118–131
 academic departments and, 121–122, 203
 approach of college, 85–86
 college major and, 137
 evaluation by, 5
 evaluation of, 26, 118–121, 130–131
 judging, 118–121, 130–131
 myths concerning, 13–14
 nature of career of, 120–121, 125–129
 organization of, 121–122, 203
 tenure track and, 122–125
 *See also* Advisers
Faulkner, William, course on, 90–99
Finances, 20–21
 of college, 203–204
 help with, 105
Financial aid office, 105
Freedom, 4, 27–28, 48
 help with problems vs., 196–198
 myth concerning, 16–17
 tenure and, 124
Friends, 22
 cult-like groups, 188–191
 dating and, 173–175, 194–195
 dormitory and, 41, 43–46

extracurricular activities and, 31, 154. *See also* Extracurricular activities
   letting go of, 186–189
   narrow focus of, 191–192
   parties and, 165–167, 186–89

Generalizing, about personal differences, 171–172
Grades, 72–74, 93
   advisers and, 110
   changing, 73–74
   meaning of, 73–74
   types of, 74
Graduate school, 126
Groupthink, 181–182

Homesickness, 19
Homophobia, 172, 176–177, 183
Honesty, 5, 6
Honors programs, 146

Identity, 175–176
Improvisation, 80–81
Independence, dormitory life and, 37–38
Independent research, 144–145
Informal advice, 114–15
Intellectual tone, of college, 6
Internships, 147

Journalism activities, 152
Journals, 83

Labs, 67, 70–71
Leadership, 3
Learning style, 3, 99
Lectures, 68–69
Library books, 50–53
Listening, 69
Literature, course in, 90–99
Loneliness, 188–191

Majors, college, 134–148
   career choice and, 137–142, 147–148
   components of, 143–146
   exploration of, 134–137
   honors in, 146
   independent research in, 144–145
   payoff from, 147–148
   selection of, 137–143
   unconventional, 146–147
Mathematics, 84–87
Minority groups
   generalizing about, 171–172
   identity and, 175–176
   personal responsibility and, 174
   stereotypes and, 172–173, 183
Myths, about college, 11–17

Note taking, 68–69, 114

Observation skills, 3
Orientation week, 37, 64, 121
Ownership, 5

Papers
   extensions on, 56, 78–79, 93
   for literature courses, 90–99
   rules concerning preparation of, 5, 50, 53–55
   *See also* Writing
Parents
   college financing by, 20–21
   expectations of, 17–19
   responsibilities of, 50–51
Parties, 165–167, 186–189
Part-time jobs, 20, 105
Peer counseling, 107
Political organizations, 153
Postponing college, 228–229
Pranks, 56–59
Prejudice, 175
Prerequisite courses, 55
President, college, 202
Privacy, 5, 29–30, 38
   confidentiality, 113
   help with problems vs., 196–198
   roommates and, 40, 42–43
Private schools, preparatory, 14–15
Professors. *See* Faculty
Property, defacing, 57–59
Psychiatrists, 105, 107
Psychologists, 105, 107

Quantitative work, 84–87
   mathematics, 84–87
   science, 85–87

Race
   generalizing about, 171–172
   identity and, 175–176
   personal responsibility and, 174
   stereotypes and, 172–173, 183
Racism, 171–172, 174–176, 183
Reading, 83–84, 222–227
   for literature courses, 90–99
   skills in, 3
Reading list, 84

Religion, 106, 113
  cult-like groups, 188–191
Research papers. *See* Papers
Resident advisers (RAs), 38, 42–43, 107
Respect, individual differences and, 174–175
Responsibility, 4, 5, 48
  discipline and, 60–62
  for personal actions, 50–51, 174
Roommates, 38–43
  difficult situations and, 39
  ground rules for, 42–43
  negotiating with, 39–43
  privacy and, 40, 42–43
  resident advisers and, 38, 42–43, 107
  safety and, 44–46
  tolerance and, 40
Rules, 48–62
  for a literature course, 92–94
  college administration and, 50, 56
  of conduct, 49–50, 56–59
  curriculum and, 50, 51, 55–56
  discipline and, 60–62, 113, 187–188
  for dormitory life, 42–43
  exceptions to, 200–201, 207
  improvising and, 80–81
  intellectual conduct and, 5, 50–55
  kinds of, 49–50
  living within, 51–55
  pranks and, 56–59
  reasons for, 49
  responsibility and. *See* Responsibility
  student government and, 205–207
  testing limits and, 55–56

Safety, dormitory, 44–46
Science, 85–87
Sections, 68
Self-analysis, 2–5
  questions for, 2–4
  in selecting a major, 136–137
  self-discovery in, 4–5
Self-image, 177
Seminars, 69, 90–99
Senior administration, 202–203
Service activities, 153
Sexism, 173, 183
  assumptions and, 177–178
  clichés and, 173–174
  respect and, 174–175

Sexual activity, 173–174, 176–177
Sexual orientation, 172, 176–177, 183
Size, of college or university, 26–28
Social life. *See* Extracurricular activities; Friends
Social organizations, 154
Special-interest groups, 153, 211–213
Sports activities, 152, 155–157
  narrow focus of, 191–192
  self-image and, 177
Standards, college admission, 31–32, 171–172
Stereotypes, 172–173, 183
Student employment office, 105
Student government, 205–207
Student opinion, 211–213
Studio courses, 71
Study groups, 44, 75
Study skills, 113–114
Success, myth of guaranteed, 12
Summer jobs, 20, 147
Syllabus, 72, 78, 92
Symbols, 224

Teachers. *See* Faculty
Tenure, 122–125
  described, 122–123
  purpose of, 124–125
Thesis, 145–146
Time management, 31, 79–80, 113–114
  extracurricular activities and, 158–160
Traditions, of college, 164–165
Trustees, college, 201–202
Tutorials, 70

Work-study programs, 105
Writing, 81–83, 222–225
  dissertation, 126
  by faculty members, 129
  journalism activities, 152
  for literature courses, 90–99
  note-taking, 68–69, 114
  skills in, 3
  sources of information and, 5
  thesis, 145–146
  *See also* Papers
Writing counselors, 104

# Other Books of Interest from the College Board

**Item Number**

003179     *Campus Health Guide*, by Carol L. Otis, M.D., and Roger Goldingay. A comprehensive medical guide, written expressly for college students, that stresses the link between a healthy lifestyle and a productive college experience. ISBN: 0-87447-317-9, $14.95

002601     *Campus Visits and College Interviews*, by Zola Dincin Schneider. An "insider's" guide to campus visits and college interviews, including 12 checklists that will help students make the most of these firsthand opportunities. ISBN: 0-87447-260-1, $9.95

003942     *The College Board Achievement Tests.* Complete and actual Achievement Tests given in 13 subjects, plus the College Board's official advice on taking the tests and sample questions from 3 new tests. ISBN: 0-87447-394-2, $12.95

003543     *The College Board Guide to Jobs and Career Planning*, by Joyce Slayton Mitchell. A guide to more than 100 careers, telling what the work is like, the education and personal skills needed, how many people are employed, where they work, and starting salaries and future employment prospects. ISBN: 0-87447-354-3, $12.95

003047     *College Bound: The Student's Handbook for Getting Ready, Moving In, and Succeeding on Campus*, by Evelyn Kaye and Janet Gardner. Help for high school seniors as they face the responsibilities and independence of being college freshmen. ISBN: 0-87447-304-7, $9.95

003756     *The College Cost Book, 1991.* A step-by-step guide to 1991 college costs and detailed financial aid for 3,100 accredited institutions. ISBN: 0-87447-375-6, $13.95 (Updated annually)

003160     *The College Guide for Parents*, by Charles J. Shields. Useful information on such topics as college choice, standardized testing, college applications, financial aid, and coping with separation anxiety. ISBN: 0-87447-316-0, $12.95

003748     *The College Handbook, 1991.* The College Board's official directory to more than 3,100 two- and four-year colleges and universities. ISBN: 0-87447-374-8, $17.95 (Updated annually)

003780     *The College Handbook for Transfer Students, 1991.* This unique directory provides students and counselors with the information they need about transfer policies at 2,800 two- and four-year colleges. ISBN: 0-87447-378-0, $14.95

003802     *The College Handbook: New England, 1991.* Complete descriptions of 233 two- and four-year institutions, plus an index of 500 majors and where they are offered. ISBN: 0-87447-380-2, $10.95

003799     *The College Handbook: New York State, 1991.* Current, detailed descriptions of New York's 256 two- and four-year colleges with a complete index of 500 majors found in New York colleges. ISBN: 0-87447-379-9, $10.95

003349     *Coping with Stress in College*, by Mark Rowh. The first book to examine the stresses specifically related to college life, this provides students with practical advice and guidelines for coping with stress. ISBN: 0-87447-334-9, $9.95

003357     *Countdown to College: Every Student's Guide to Getting the Most Out of High School*, by Zola Dincin Schneider and Phyllis B. Kalb. A one-of-a-kind book to help every teenager do well in high school and be prepared for college. ISBN: 0-87447-335-7, $9.95.

| | |
|---|---|
| 003055 | *How to Help Your Teenager Find the Right Career*, by Charles J. Shields. Step-by-step advice and innovative ideas to help parents motivate their children to explore careers and find alternatives suited to their interests and abilities. ISBN: 0-87447-305-5, $12.95 |
| 002482 | *How to Pay for Your Children's College Education*, by Gerald Krefetz. Practical advice to help parents of high school students, as well as of young children, finance their children's college education. ISBN: 0-87447-248-2, $12.95 |
| 003764 | *Index of Majors, 1991*. Lists over 500 majors at the 3,000 colleges and graduate institutions, state by state, that offer them. ISBN: 0-87447-376-4, $14.95 (Updated annually) |
| 003950 | *The Revised College Board Guide to the CLEP Examinations*. Provides expert advice on how to find out which colleges grant credit for CLEP, decide which examinations to take, prepare for the CLEP examinations, and interpret the scores. ISBN: 0-87447-395-0, $11.95 |
| 003535 | *The Student's Guide to Good Writing*, by Rick Dalton and Marianne Dalton, Guidelines and detailed information on how to meet the challenges of writing assignments for *all* college courses. ISBN: 0-87447-353-5, $9.95 |
| 002598 | *Succeed with Math*, by Sheila Tobias. A *practical* guide that helps students overcome math anxiety and gives them the tools for mastering the subject in high school and college courses as well as the world of work. ISBN: 0-87447-259-8, $12.95 |
| 003225 | *Summer on Campus*, by Shirley Levin. A comprehensive guide to more than 250 summer programs at over 150 universities. ISBN: 0-87447-322-5, $9.95 |
| 003667 | *10 SATs: Fourth Edition*. Ten actual, recently administered SATs plus the full text of *Taking the SAT*, the College Board's official advice. ISBN: 0-87447-366-7, $11.95 |
| 002571 | *Writing Your College Application Essay*, by Sarah Myers McGinty. An informative and reassuring book that helps students write distinctive application essays and explains what colleges are looking for in these essays. ISBN: 0-87447-257-1, $9.95 |
| 002474 | *Your College Application*, by Scott Gelband, Catherine Kubale, and Eric Schorr. A step-by-step guide to help students do their best on college applications. ISBN: 0-87447-247-4, $9.95 |

To order by direct mail any books or software not available in your local store, please specify the title and item number and send your request with a check made payable to the College Board for the full amount plus $2.95 for handling to: College Board Publications, Box 886, New York, New York 10101-0886. The College Board pays fourth-class book rate postage. Allow 30 days from receipt of order for delivery. An institutional purchase order (for a minimum of $25) is required in order to be billed, and fourth-class book rate postage plus $2.95 for handling will be charged on all billed orders.

To charge your purchase to Visa or MasterCard (minimum of $14.95 plus $2.95 for handling), call 1/800/323-7155 Monday through Thursday, 8 AM to 12 midnight; Friday, 8 AM to 11 PM EST. Shipment is by UPS at College Board expense.